GPS FOR GRADUATE SCHOOL
Students Share Their Stories

D0880167

GPS FOR GRADUATE SCHOOL
Students Share Their Stories

EDITED BY MARK J. T. SMITH
with contributions from M. M. Browne, Kiana R. Johnson, and William J. Peck

Purdue University Press, West Lafayette, Indiana

Library of Congress Cataloging-in-Publication Data

GPS for graduate school : students share their stories / [21 authors] ; Edited by Mark J. T. Smith.

    pages cm

  Includes bibliographical references.

  ISBN 978-1-55753-674-7 (pbk. : alk. paper) — ISBN 978-1-61249-313-8 (epdf) — ISBN 978-1-61249-314-5 (epub) 1. Universities and college—Graduate work—Handbooks, manuals, etc. 2. Graduate students—United States—Handbooks, manuals, etc. I. Smith, Mark J. T., editor.

  LB2371.4.G67 2014

  378.1'55—dc23

                  2013042313

Some names have been changed to protect the privacy of the individuals involved.

Contents

Foreword

It is no secret that the United States is not producing enough graduates with doctoral degrees in science, technology, engineering, and math—commonly referred to as the STEM fields—to meet its needs in the twenty-first century. Reports from Educational Testing Service and the Council of Graduate Schools, among many other organizations and associations, have detailed the critical shortage of STEM graduates and its potential threat to the competitiveness of the United States. In an effort to address the problem in the Indiana–Chicago Midwest sector, three premier universities—Indiana University, Northwestern University, and Purdue University—have joined forces to create the Midwest Crossroads Alliance for Graduate Education and the Professoriate (AGEP). The overarching goals of the Midwest Crossroads AGEP are to create an infrastructure within and across the three universities for attracting undergraduates to its STEM graduate programs and to prepare its graduate students for successful careers in the professoriate.

The Midwest Crossroads AGEP is deeply committed to preparing its students for success in the professoriate. During its five years of funding by the National Science Foundation, it has worked diligently to create programs and initiatives that provide students with opportunities to augment their academic training, professional development, and networks beyond what is available in their respective programs or institutions. This inter-institutional collaboration enables select students in STEM fields to reap invaluable experiences that enhance their education, job search, and career preparation.

This edited book is but one example of the unique opportunities provided by the Midwest Crossroads AGEP. The purpose of this project is to give students from various STEM disciplines an occasion to collaborate on a major enterprise that fosters teambuilding and writing skills, both of which are essential for success in the professoriate. Through contributing chapters to this volume, interested students learn about the processes involved in jointly authoring a book and having their work critiqued by professional coaches. In addition, the authors make a lasting contribution that is likely to be an inspiration to graduate students not just in the Midwest Crossroads AGEP, but also those in other AGEP Alliances and graduate programs throughout the country.

This undertaking has imparted to its student authors lessons in the steps involved in writing many of the types of books one would expect to see in STEM fields and, perhaps more importantly, has enabled them to enhance their writing techniques and develop interpersonal skills that are essential for successful partnerships in research. Graduate students quickly comprehend once beginning their programs of study that writing is a necessary requirement for being a member of the academy, and even more, that often it takes time to learn and develop strong writing skills. Those in the STEM disciplines are also beginning to understand that the model of a faculty member working alone in her or his office is frequently too inefficient, particularly as projects increasingly become more complex and interdisciplinary in scope. Of course, the success of this book project is for readers to judge, but the efforts of its authors make it clear that the Midwest Crossroads AGEP is accomplishing its objective: students are cultivating professional development experiences in writing and collaboration that will prepare them for productive careers in the professoriate.

The Midwest Crossroads AGEP has not been in existence long, yet in all three institutions out of which it operates, it has developed infrastructure and increased both enrollments and the number of its students who graduate. Its students have worked together within and across all three campuses. This edited book is one of the most visible examples of the achievements resulting from this inter-institutional collaboration. The Midwest Crossroads AGEP is happy to have sponsored this project and is grateful to the students who chose to participate.

James C. Wimbush
Dean of the University Graduate School and Professor of Business Administration
Indiana University

Preface

Few people are aware of how many doctoral students actually finish their PhD program. Completion rates vary wildly from university to university. Some are high. Some are low. But on average, the PhD completion rate is less than 60 percent in the United States, according to the Council of Graduate Schools. This book, devoted to providing a PhD road map to graduation, is the first of its kind. That's not to say there aren't scores of books on the market that discuss how to be successful in graduate school. But what makes this book unique and appealing is its approach to the subject—an approach best appreciated by understanding how it came to be.

This book is a product of the Midwest Crossroads Alliance for Graduate Education and the Professoriate (AGEP)—an alliance of Indiana University, Northwestern University, and Purdue University. The goal of the Midwest Crossroads AGEP is to increase the number of underrepresented students who graduate with PhDs in the science, technology, engineering, and mathematics (STEM) fields. One of its activities is the Northwestern University–initiated book club, which has expanded across the Midwest Crossroads AGEP. Students and faculty meet regularly in small groups to discuss books about graduate school, typically reviewing a different chapter at each meeting. Inspired by the book club experience, we considered during one of the Alliance conferences having our AGEP students write an edited book that could be used as source material for a book club discussion or seminar series. The idea was received with great enthusiasm by everyone. Recognizing the magnitude of experiential wisdom among our AGEP students, we launched the project. After approximately three years of writing, editing, and revising, the project is now complete. This book contains ten chapters written by sixteen graduate student authors and two AGEP-affiliated academic professionals from across the Alliance, with the assistance of two writing coaches: Mary Maxine Browne and William J. Peck.

In writing this book, we assumed that many readers would be senior undergraduate and graduate students who would read the book individually. But most interesting to us was creating a product that also would be ideal for a seminar or book club application in which a facilitator would lead chapter discussions with a group of students. Because we noticed a void in books written with this goal in mind, we paid careful attention to customizing the book to serve those interested in having discussions about topics related to graduate school. In particular, we created brief video vignettes based on the chapter themes with accompanying discussion activities, an approach that encourages participants to have an in-depth and fruitful discussion of the chapter content. The combination of the chapters with their videos and support materials sets this book apart from other books on success in graduate school. As a whole, it equips facilitators to lead lively and thought-provoking discussions on the issues presented in the various chapters.

The chapter topics address the following: obtaining fellowship support, managing the challenges of the first year of graduate school, finding a thesis advisor, working with thesis committee members, balancing family and graduate student life, establishing collaborations, seeking academic support, publishing, and planning for life after graduate school. While treatments of these issues can be found in other texts by accomplished scholars, this book employs personal narratives as the vehicle to convey the challenges one can face in graduate school. Our AGEP chapter authors were encouraged to draw on their personal experience and exercise poetic license in writing their narratives to make them as relevant and interesting as possible.

As with any project of this type, many people contributed along the way. We are grateful to Dean James Wimbush at Indiana University and Dean Dwight McBride at Northwestern for their support of the Midwest Crossroads AGEP program and appreciate the general assistance we received from our Alliance staff members: Cheryl Judice, Maxine Watson, Yolanda Treviño, Kathy Dixon, Penny Warren, NaShara Mitchell, and Kiersti Cunningham.

In the early phases of this book project, we benefited from stimulating discussions with Barbara Schwom and the unfaltering leadership of AGEP scholar Kiana R. Johnson, who was instrumental in keeping the troops on task. Deserving special recognition are Mary Maxine Browne and William J. Peck, both of whom invested many hours as writing coaches, helping our authors develop their narratives and drafting the original script ideas for the video vignettes.

During the final year of the project, Mary Maxine coordinated the last phases of the book's completion. She also organized graduate student sessions to test and revise the activity materials and served as project manager for the video recordings, collaborating with videographer Jason Doty. The creation of the videos benefited tremendously from Jason's exceptional directing and video production skills. We are also grateful to Lisa Hilliard for providing closed captioning for the videos.

Finally, we enthusiastically acknowledge the AGEP students, summer students, Indiana Louis Stokes Alliance for Minority Participation (LSAMP) students, and faculty facilitators who participated in reviewing and critiquing the discussion materials and video vignettes. We have enjoyed our interactions with all the students, staff, and faculty members who have touched this project and are grateful for their participation. We are convinced that you, as a reader of this edited volume, will benefit from the insights and perspectives of our AGEP students as we have over the years.

Mark J. T. Smith
Dean of the Graduate School and Michael and Katherine Birck Professor
of Electrical and Computer Engineering
Purdue University

Lawrence J. Henschen
Professor of Electrical Engineering and Computer Science
Northwestern University

Facilitating the Chapter Discussions

This book was developed with the idea that advisors, mentors, or groups of students may wish to use the chapters as source material for discussions about graduate school as part of a seminar or ongoing book discussion group. A *Facilitator's Guide* is available for each chapter with step-by-step instructions on leading the discussions. We also have created short videos with closed captioning, one for each chapter, along with accompanying discussion questions and activities. All of these materials are available online. At the end of each chapter, you will find the URL for a resource web page, from which you can download the *Facilitator's Guide*, the video, and activity materials. We recommend that facilitators download the video and supporting materials in advance of the discussion session.

Different from typical educational videos, the videos presented here depict a scenario in which graduate students are confronted with a problem based on the themes of the corresponding chapter. Each video ends in a cliffhanger, which leaves the problem unsolved, giving the audience the opportunity to discuss and participate in group activities to find solutions. This process leads the participants into a tangible experience of graduate school life and offers insights into the management of a successful graduate career.

The videos bring to life the topics addressed in the book chapters and spark the participants' interest so that they can engage in discussions that are informative and rewarding. The discussion questions and group activities challenge the participants to think through the problems facing the characters in the videos, thereby giving the participants a real taste of the graduate school experience. Every group, however, differs in terms of the personalities of its members. Where one group can be very open and verbally gregarious, the next group can be shy and less talkative. It is with various group constellations in mind that we have provided different types of discussion materials for group facilitators to choose from, so that they can tailor their use of this book to the needs and preferences of their students.

The *Facilitator's Guide* associated with each chapter provides an easy-to-use script for leading an engaging chapter discussion. All of these guides have the same organizational pattern and begin with discussion questions that address the content of the book chapter. The video portion begins with reading a video synopsis. The group then watches the video and afterward participants discuss questions provided to help them more fully understand the problem facing the characters. If the accompanying activities are to be used, the facilitator introduces the problem-solving activity using the materials that have been downloaded and printed out in advance of the session. The activities vary from chapter to chapter and can involve role-plays, data gathering, interviews, mock proposals, and large and small group discussions, depending on the particular chapter. Working with the discussion questions, watching the video, and completing the group activities takes approximately fifty minutes. The session length can vary depending on the length of the discussions. If a shorter session is needed, we suggest that just the video introduction, the video, and its discussion questions be used together. We have tried to make all of these materials easily accessible and user friendly. The activities have been carefully designed by a team of AGEP (Alliance for Graduate Education and the Professoriate) graduate students with the goal of fully engaging the participants in the topic under discussion. All of the activities have been tested and fine-tuned with groups of graduate students at Purdue University in preparation for their inclusion in this book.

Chapter 1

Locating and Securing Funding

Delia S. Shelton

◄───►

INTRODUCTION

Nationwide tuition hikes and reductions in state and federal aid can be a source of worry for graduate students. At the same time, graduate education can be made affordable with access to the proper resources. There are over 2.4 million scholarships and grants, worth in excess of $15 billion, available every year to fund graduate level education. While the availability of these scholarships and grants is a boon for students, it also raises a problem. Applying for scholarships and grants takes time and energy, so students have to determine which funding sources are right for them and worth their time and energy and also consider how their goals and strengths fit with the priorities and values of each funding agency.

This chapter provides examples of and suggestions for how to secure funding. In my account of my battle with the beast, the National Science Foundation (NSF) Graduate Research Fellowship Program (GRFP) application,

I recount the unforeseen challenges that required me to respond quickly and remain proactive for not one but two application cycles. Further, I demonstrate that my success was contingent on my diligent quest for secondary education support, turning it from an arduous and mundane task into a well-planned self-reflective adventure.

INITIATING THE SEARCH FOR FUNDING RESOURCES

Obtaining monetary support for your graduate education involves a number of considerations, and the decisions you make are fully dependent upon your academic and career goals, academic status, and sources of funding. For instance, the funding opportunities for, resources needed by, and objectives of a student who is just entering graduate school differ radically from those of either an individual who is already dissertating or a postdoctoral fellow. That said, prior to beginning your search for funding sources, you need to organize your thoughts and clearly define your aims. Contemplate the intentions of the funds: will they be used for living expenses, conference travel, or research endeavors?

After identifying the purpose of your funding, you need to reflect on the personal traits and qualities that make you a desirable candidate to funding agencies. More specifically, you need to consider how these attributes will align with the missions of the different granting agencies. In other words, you need to think from the perspective of the institution. For instance, ask yourself: "What do they have to gain by selecting me, and how does awarding me this fellowship help fulfill their mission and goals?" Understanding the mindset of the granting institution is, of course, important during the search process, but it is crucial in the application process. This insight will put you in a position that will increase your prospects of securing funding.

The next pre-search step involves both defining your field of interest and creating an exhaustive list of all key terms that could be associated with your specialized area. You can use an extensive list of terms to search for a broad range of funding sources applicable to your field of interest. The last step in the pre-search process is to identify what you want to accomplish by obtaining the funding. Is the funding intended to cover the entirety of a project, to fund your graduate program, or solely to defray the cost of your attendance at a conference?

Once you have outlined your thoughts and objectives regarding your search for funding, you are now ready to begin the expedition to find pots of gold that will support you in your graduate studies. A plethora of resources are available to help you locate and identify funding sources, and your personal connections and relationships, as well as basic research skills, will help you identify appropriate funding sources for your studies. The most important resource for locating and securing funding is people. Professors and advisors have both searched for funding themselves and guided other students in this quest. They can point you in the right direction to start your search.

Finally, this can never be said enough: *The early bird gets the worm.* To find gold at the end of the application rainbow, you need to begin your search as early as possible. Over 65 percent of all fellowship application deadlines fall between October and March, and the number one reason individuals are rejected is that they fail to meet the application deadline. In the narrative that follows, I recount my experience as a young scholar with what I call "the beast," the NSF GRFP application, and show that my knowledge from my undergraduate degree as well as my persistence and hard work were paramount to my eventual success.

> *A little more persistence, a little more effort, and what seemed hopeless failure may turn to glorious success.*
>
> ELBERT HUBBARD (1856–1915)

My quest for financial support spanned nearly two years of relentless searching, nights of agonizing editing, moments of inspiration, and fist-clenching triumph. As an aspiring academic, I had set many goals for myself. I wanted to pursue a doctorate in animal behavior in order to identify the mechanisms underlying the emergent group phenomenon. My goal, which spurred my ambition, was to acquire funding so that I could complete my degree while being indebted to none save for humanity. I am happy to say that to this day my only debts are to humanity, because "to whom much is given much is required," and that my successful search for fellowships left me financially in the clear.

As an undergraduate, my academic advisor suggested that I add receiving an NSF GRFP award to my long list of academic ambitions. My toil with the NSF GRFP application spanned nearly two years, three countries, hundreds of correspondences, and a multitude of drafts. Although my struggle was compounded by living in another country, my essays were enriched by spending my senior year abroad in countries where technological communication devices were luxuries and general access was limited. Under these conditions, the NSF's fully electronic application process was daunting to say the least.

I began working seriously on my fellowship application two months prior to the deadline, while I was an exchange student at Universidad Nacional located in Heredia, Costa Rica. In hindsight, given the circumstances, I should have started much earlier.

On the day I buckled down in front of a Spanish language keyboard, I found that locating the NSF GRFP web page was a simple task, but interpreting the two criteria of evaluation it listed, Intellectual Merit and Broader Impacts, was mystifying. In my initial drafts, I made the mistake of consulting a good old friend, Merriam-Webster, for insights rather than the NSF materials themselves. In my first attempt at the application, I tried to explain that I was a child prodigy like Albert Einstein. This draft resulted in little other than my academic advisor's comedic critique, after which I thought deeply and remembered my undergraduate training.

First and foremost, I remembered that I always need to consult the primary literature, which, though it may take some perseverance, will reveal the author's, or in this case the agency's, intended meaning. Second, I remembered a concept I learned in one of my psychology classes: *umwelt*. An Estonian biologist named Jakob von Uexküll used the German word *umwelt* to refer to the perceptual world of organisms or the sort of self-world in which organisms exist and perceive their surroundings. He suggested that the self-worlds of animals differ radically from those of humans and only in considering these perceptual differences could we truly understand the lives of these animals. In remembering this concept, I realized that the administrators who read my application would likely have a different set of values and goals than did I as a student, especially in terms of what they would laud in applicants. It occurred to me that I should market my application not from my perspective, but from the perspective of the granting agency. Specifically, I should compose my application such that I not only address the criteria but also embody the mission, the *umwelt*, of the National Science Foundation.

I quickly applied my research skills to the application process. I wanted to garner as much information on writing a successful proposal as possible so I could establish a plan of action for the application process. I found the reviews written by experienced applicants and reviewers instrumental in this pursuit. I scoured the NSF FastLane website, YouTube, university websites, and blogspots not only for probing self-reflective questions but also for model essays. Surprisingly, YouTube has quite a few clips on the NSF GRFP. I was able to find clips of NSF representatives speaking at different institutions around the country about the GRFP. The representatives provided useful tips and a reviewer's perspective of the application process. My search of blog posts and university websites informed my decision regarding who to select to write my letters of recommendation.

My various readings, YouTube videos, and communications with my academic advisor helped me grasp the meaning of the NSF criteria Intellectual Merit and Broader Impacts. So when I began writing, I was able to approach the keyboard with meaningful definitions of those criteria, as well as ideas about how to incorporate concretely in my essays the many ways I would fulfill them. For me, Broader Impacts was how my work and explicit actions would positively affect my community. A community is composed of many mutually inclusive parts. In the case of the academic community as it applied to my work, these parts consisted of special interest groups (e.g., conservationists excited about preserving endangered fish species, otherwise known as aquaculturists), undergraduates, secondary and primary school students, and underrepresented groups, which I vowed to mentor and include in my research. Reading diverse essays and skimming editorials on the "dos and don'ts" of essay writing allowed me to hone my intellectual voice, which I then used to compose a set of concise and cogent essays that embodied my purpose and the mission of the NSF.

Ordering academic transcripts is also an important part of preparing to apply for funding, but it seemed like a menial task to me. As I progressed further into my application process, I kicked myself for not ordering my transcripts earlier. I faced some difficulty in getting my transcripts because I had attended two institutions during my undergraduate career. Luckily, I had mass-ordered transcripts from one institution earlier in the year. For the second one, I relied purely on the loving-kindness of my father, the speed of my small institution, and pure luck. I sent an e-mail to my father, asking if he could go in person to retrieve my transcripts for me. My parents lived just two hours from this school, so my father was able to drive there and personally request the transcripts on my behalf. Even then, unexpected paperwork issues presented themselves, such as the need for a signature and at least a two-hour wait for transcripts. Had the school been larger and its rules more stringent, it could have taken a week to fulfill my request and another week for the transcripts to arrive at the funding agency, which would have caused me to miss the deadline. Fortunately for me, my father was able to get the transcripts I needed and overnight them to me.

Requesting letters of recommendation is another important step in preparing to apply for funding. In the midst of self-reflection, intermittent writing, and the exploration of cloud forests in Costa Rica, a discomforting question became more foreboding and imminent. I had pushed the question of who I should ask to write a letter of recommendation under rotting plantain peels long enough. The guidelines stated I could ask up to eight individuals but needed a minimum of four letters on file. I knew I could easily fill three of the slots: two from members of my undergraduate thesis committee with whom I had an outstanding professional relationship and a third from a research scientist at Merck Research Laboratories with whom I was collaboratively writing a paper for publication in *Behavioral Brain Research*. I composed a cheerful e-mail to each of these prospective recommenders in which I detailed my reason for contacting them and told them about my academic experiences in Costa Rica. At the bottom of the e-mail, I inserted the NSF criteria and attached my resume and an unfinished but cohesive draft of my personal statement.

Self-denigration, resistance, and procrastination began to creep into my thinking, which cast a shadow on the rest of the application process. It was two weeks later, and I had yet to decide firmly from whom I would request the required fourth letter of recommendation. I was trying to decide between two possible recommenders. My dilemma was whether I should request a letter from a mentor I had known for several years who was well acquainted with my outreach activities but limited in her knowledge of my research endeavors, or from a scientific superstar I had met only a handful of times. I was a little uncertain about the scientific superstar as one of my recommenders because I was not completely convinced he knew me well enough to write a strong recommendation. However, I was enthralled with the fantasy of his writing a positive letter that would be a magnificent recommendation and completely convince the review committee to accept my application.

On the other hand, I kept replaying in my mind the words of advice I had received—that it is better to have a strong letter of recommendation from a little-known voice than a vague recommendation from a well-known voice. On top of that, I was also trying to decide how many letters I should request. In my pondering, I convinced myself that many strong letters would overpower the single questionably positive and vague letter of recommendation I might get from the scientific superstar. So I gambled a little and came to the haphazard conclusion that *more* recommenders would be my best strategy. Thus, I requested letters from both prospective recommenders.

I received confirmations from four out of my five recommenders about two weeks after I requested their support. The remaining recommender, my advisor, whose letter I thought would impact my application in the most positive manner, required quite a bit of prodding, a lesson I learned too late in some of my concurrent graduate applications. I was a nervous wreck when I examined the reference page, two days before the letter of recommendation deadline, and found that my academic advisor had yet to submit a letter. Nevertheless, I calmly collected my thoughts and wrote a concerned e-mail to my advisor reminding him of the deadline and inquiring about any action I could take to facilitate the process. The following day, he apologized for the delay, thanked me for the reminder, and sent the letter on time.

> *Procrastination is the enemy. The application*
> *process is not over until a "submit confirmation"*
> *receipt is printed, and in the meantime, anything*
> *that can go wrong will go wrong.*

As the submission deadline neared, I dramatically shifted my schedule so I could dedicate more time to the application. Nevertheless, my procrastination caught up with me. My schedule overhaul did not save me from a race with the clock, a virtual virus, or an overwhelmed server. An unforeseen virus that resulted in the complete destruction of my computer left me devastated. This experience affirmed the value in saving files frequently and in multiple locations.

Three days before the deadline, I was fervently writing and editing with great success. However, I knew my weary eyes were not keen enough to catch simple grammatical mistakes. I needed another set of eyes, but my poor time management left me with few options. I shamefacedly asked my mother to edit my three 2,000-word essays the day before they were due. Although she obliged, she scolded me. Her castigating words of wisdom resonate with me still today: my inadequate planning shows poor time management and a lack of respect for others' time. Fortunately my mother saved me and I had edited copies of my essays in my hands in time to meet the deadline.

I completed the final edits two hours before the 5:00 p.m. deadline, but I was having no success uploading the application to the NSF website. Error messages continually popped up all over my computer screen. I tried three separate computers in the overcrowded Universidad Nacional computer lab with similar and frustrating results. I concluded that I had a malfunctioning Internet connection. My failed attempts cost me precious time. I had thirty minutes to download three separate files from my e-mail account, log in to an overtaxed FastLane account, upload each separate document file, and press the submit button. I realized at that moment that my allegiance to procrastination might have just cost me a fellowship.

With hopes of a miracle, I ran frantically to the closest Internet café to submit my application. My calm nearly disintegrated into mass hysteria as the digital computer clock rolled to 5:00. I collected my last seeds of rational thought, launched my Skype account and dialed the NSF technical helpline from memory. I waited with my heart racing, as the busy signal rang in my ear again and again. I called probably thirty to forty times, because it was one of those hit or miss busy signals. Either you made contact with a representative or you didn't and had to hang up and try again. Finally, after at least a half an hour of trying, I made contact with the helpline. I explained my dilemma feverishly to the representative. His words, "The server is down; submit your application ASAP," were like a breath of fresh air and propelled me through the next set of hurdles.

I raced to the next nearest Internet café, still trying to find a reliable Internet connection, came up with an irrational idea, and made several foolish decisions, further jeopardizing my chances of winning a fellowship and putting myself at risk for identity theft. As my computer struggles continued and I went further and further past the 5:00 p.m. deadline, I began to worry I was exceeding the NSF's extra allowance due to their server problems. A girl in my exchange program was from Hawaii, where the time was four hours earlier than in Costa Rica. I asked her if she knew someone who could log in to my account, upload my essays, and submit my application. She sympathized with me and agreed to assist me in my crazy attempts at submitting my application to the NSF on time.

She gave me the phone number and e-mail address of a friend of hers. My attempts to make contact with her friend were futile. So, I logged into a Hawaii chat system and explained my circumstance to flirting strangers. My pleas were met with snarky remarks and laughter. At 7:45 p.m. I relinquished my irrational idea, which wouldn't have worked anyway because as I learned later, NSF deadlines do not alter with time zones. I loaded the essays and pressed the submit button, sank down in my chair of desolation, and realized procrastination had defeated me. I was fully prepared to receive an immediate rejection by e-mail:

> *Dear Ms. Shelton,*
>
> *You failed to submit your application by the designated deadline. Your application will not be considered for funding. Please, apply again next year.*
>
> *NSF Program Officer*

Two weeks after I submitted my NSF application, I had yet to receive such an e-mail. I called the NSF hotline and was elated to find that my application had been accepted. I thanked a higher power and pledged to change my work habits immediately.

> *When you make a mistake, don't look back at it long. Take the reason of the thing into your mind and then look forward. Mistakes are lessons of wisdom. The past cannot be changed. The future is yet in your power.*
>
> Hugh White (1773–1840)

Six months later and three weeks after the official announcement, I was notified while in Ghana that I had been awarded an Honorable Mention. Although I should have been proud of my efforts, I was angered and disheartened, especially after reading the reviewers' comments. There was great discrepancy between two of the three reviewers. The third reviewer's comments appeared as though he or she hadn't read my application or had copied and pasted comments from a different application by accident. I soothed my bitterness by basking in the sun and jumping in the waves of the Gold Coast beach.

Upon my return to the United States and following my re-acclimation to the environment and culture back home, I clicked on the link that sent me virtually to the reviewers' comments. Although fire swelled in my veins, this time it sparked determination rather than anger. I read the reviewers' comments with the goal of understanding each one's *umwelt* and the ways in which I could improve my application for the next vie for NSF gold. I poured over each paragraph, making notes of each line of constructive criticism. Some of the conclusions I gleaned from their remarks were that the Broader Impacts section of my application could use some sprucing, the applicable importance of my research proposal was lacking, and I needed to consult a phylogeneticist, an expert who studies evolutionary relatedness among groups of organisms, on the appropriateness of the model organism I had proposed. I coupled these points of consideration with a tough lesson learned—procrastination is a formidable force to be reckoned with—and I put a concerted effort into applying again. I had lost a lot that year, but gained much more in experience.

> *She had an unequalled gift . . . of squeezing big*
> *mistakes into small opportunities.*
>
> HENRY JAMES (1843–1916)

I decided to forego attending graduate school the year after my undergraduate studies, and instead I enrolled in an alternative teaching certification program. I taught integrated physics and chemistry at an inner city Title 1 high school. My first two months of teaching presented challenges that earned the task of teaching science to high school students the honor of being the hardest I had signed up for to date. In the end, though, my experience as a teacher made me a more compassionate and knowledgeable individual and consequently helped me make my next NSF application even stronger.

After sprucing up my essays with my impactful teaching experience, I spammed friends and family with my personal statement and previous research essays, asking for their feedback, which I gratefully received. During the summer, I sent my research proposal essay to every appropriate contact I met at conferences. I even boldly requested feedback from phylogeneticists and ichthyologists I had never met. Some ignored my correspondence, but the majority of them were helpful and some went to the great lengths of tediously editing my proposal. On the day that the NSF FastLane opened for applications, I requested letters of recommendation from the three individuals, the minimum requirement that year, who were most acquainted with my goals and aspirations and could speak to my Broader Impacts and Intellectual Merit in detail. The NSF received my transcripts a month before the application closed and I submitted my completed application a full three weeks before the deadline. You could say I didn't take any chances the second time around. I gathered my materials for a single slingshot to success.

Let the waiting game continue, but be proactive.

Rather than putting all my eggs in one basket, as I had done during the previous application cycle, this time I applied not only to the NSF but also for multiple fellowships, using my well-written NSF essays as the basis for my other application essays. In April and May, I was elated to find I had been awarded three fellowships, including the NSF Graduate Research Fellowship Program (GRFP). I used my hefty funding packages to barter with the universities from whom I had received acceptance letters. My hard work paid off, and I elatedly matriculated into a PhD program the following fall, fully funded for five years. With this level of financial security I purchased a home, but that is a discussion for another chapter.

CONCLUSION

The fellowship application process provides an opportunity for self-reflection. I found the process of soliciting feedback on essays humbling. In addition, requesting letters of recommendation revived and strengthened my connections with mentors, advisors, and supervisors and showed me how important it is to maintain connections for future support. Additionally, I learned what I was capable of under pressure, and that *no* means *new opportunity.* In all, the process demonstrated to me that my experiences both inside and outside the classroom have shaped and influenced me greatly, and that sharing my story with a more general audience is a skill that requires practice. Moreover, I have learned that many struggles can be overcome simply with a well-defined plan and by avoiding procrastination.

CHAPTER 1 GROUP DISCUSSION

Securing an external fellowship requires determination, planning, and effort, as illustrated in Delia's story. Her experiences and the winning approach she describes can serve as a road map for anyone interested in applying for a competitive fellowship or grant. While the applicant's perspective is obviously beneficial to students planning to write fellowship and grant proposals, the perspective of the agency that will be making the award decision is also helpful to understand. Sharing thoughts and ideas in a group discussion about how to write a proposal can improve your chances for success.

The video for this chapter, titled *Inside the Forum*, takes you behind the scenes, where you observe members of a funding panel debate the pros and cons of two highly competitive student grant applications. After viewing the video, you will have the opportunity to apply the insights you've gleaned from both the chapter and the video by developing your own proposal. The video and accompanying materials for leading a group discussion on this chapter can be downloaded from the chapter 1 resource web page at http://dx.doi.org/10.5703/1288284315197.

CHAPTER AUTHOR PROFILE

Delia S. Shelton

Following her father's military service, Ms. Shelton grew up in a small rural town in Texas. Her fondness for animals and science was cultivated via her participation in 4-H and math and science programs. She was fortunate to encounter wonderful, enduring mentors who cultivated her professional development. She completed her undergraduate degree in animal behavior and Spanish at Southwestern University in Texas. She later continued her education at Indiana University in Bloomington, where she is currently working toward her PhD. Like many students, Ms. Shelton would never have been able to enter these degree programs without financial assistance. Creativity and guidance permitted her to garner nearly half million dollars in fellowships and scholarships, including a National Science Foundation (NSF) Graduate Research Fellowship (GRFP award) and an NSF Integrative Graduate Education and Research Traineeship (IGERT) award.

Chapter 2

The First Year of Graduate School: Navigating the Hurdles

Christy L. Erving
Lauren J. Parker
Jamelle K. P. Williams, PhD
Sean A. Colbert-Kelly, PhD

INTRODUCTION

Many students walk onto campus on their first day of graduate school feeling incredibly nervous, often having no conception of the challenges that lie ahead. This chapter discusses some of the hurdles that first-year graduate students encounter: the highs and lows, the unexpected twists and turns, disappointing downturns, and proud successes. Making it through the first year is often an indicator of the successful completion of the degree, so maintaining a positive attitude in the first two terms is important. With patience and perseverance, the rough spots of the first year are surmountable and success in the end can be achieved. In this chapter Christy, Lauren, Jamelle, and Sean relate some of their experiences establishing themselves in their departments, managing coursework and teaching responsibilities, and dealing with qualifying exams. Their stories describe the challenges they met and the hurdles they navigated during their first year of graduate school.

ENTERING THE GRADUATE SCHOOL ENVIRONMENT: ESTABLISHING YOUR BRAND FOR SUCCESS

Often the graduate school "brand" you forge is made not so much by how you deal with successes, but how you manage the challenges in the first year of the graduate program. The way in which you pick yourself up and keep going in the face of difficulties, especially during the first year of a graduate program, establishes a professional base that can serve to help or hinder your progress through graduate school. What does it actually mean to *establish your brand?* Your brand tells people who you are, your communication style, and your standards. The way you interact with your graduate student colleagues and professors establishes your brand in your work environment—in this case, your graduate program. It lets people know what to expect from you. As the narratives which follow relate, establishing yourself as a person of high integrity and reliability in your department will open lines of communication with people who can help further your career in terms of professional networking, references, and opportunities.

Suddenly Immersed, Gradually Successful

Once she was established in her graduate program, with hard work and determination Christy became a successful student, teacher, and researcher. The initial adjustment to graduate school was a challenge, however. During her first year, she struggled to maintain confidence in her knowledge and her ability to relate her ideas to others in the department. Though Christy knew that pursuing a doctoral degree was the only way to accomplish her dream of becoming a professor, she was not sure she could cut it—that she was strong enough and smart enough to match the competition. Fortunately her commitment to succeed was strong, and so she found a way to strengthen her ability to communicate with her peers and instructors. Through her consistent participation in the face of her own fears, she established her brand as a valued contributor to the scholarly conversation in her department who was welcomed and appreciated for her thoughts and ideas. This accomplishment didn't come overnight, however, as she describes in her story.

Christy: Early on in the first semester of the first year of my graduate program at Indiana University, I struggled with feelings of low self-confidence. There I was at a major university, and I was expected to teach, to write papers that would be published in nationally read journals, and to prepare a dissertation research project. All of this seemed way beyond me, and then I made an even more daunting discovery: I was expected to participate in the Social Psychology, Health, and the Life Course Workshop, more commonly known as the SHeL seminar. This departmental seminar is held every week in the fall semester, and no doubt is left in the minds of the graduate students in the Department of Sociology as to whether or not they need to be there. It is not a course requirement, but as I will relate, missing it would definitely be a step down on one's career ladder in the department. E-mails announcing the workshop topic along with strong encouragement to attend appeared in my in-box during the first week of classes. Despite its publicity, I was tempted to forego this meeting since I figured I was too new and too unfamiliar with the field to attend. However, this notion was quickly corrected when I ran into my advisor on the day of the first SHeL workshop and she asked me if I was planning to attend. Now, I had heard that she was in charge of the SHeL seminar, but I didn't think that it meant she would expect me, the newbie, to actually be there. Well, I was wrong.

As she approached me, she said, "Hello there, Christy. How are you doing today? You are going to be at the SHeL today, aren't you?" I swallowed my natural response, which was something like, *Who, me?* and instead said brightly, "Of course. I wouldn't miss it." She smiled and replied, "Good. I look forward to seeing you. Don't forget your lunch."

Though I had just promised to attend the SHeL workshop, I had a nagging thought that I was forgetting some other obligation. Then it came to me: I had been assigned a take-home test for my social theory course which was due at the same time as the workshop. In fact, this take-home test was a substantial portion of my final grade in the class, so it could not be turned in late. In order to make it on time to the workshop, I rushed back to the lab, worked like lightning, and just barely managed to get my test done on time. Then I hurried back down the hall to the workshop. I was the last one in the door. As I sat down I realized I had forgotten several bare essentials, like a pen and paper to take notes, and my lunch. I hoped my advisor would think I had eaten really fast.

Once I got over the fact that I was grossly ill-prepared for the workshop, I relaxed a little. Many of my fellow graduate students and faculty members were there, all seemingly eager to present and share their research with each other. They seemed perfectly happy that a new first-year graduate student like me was sitting there with them (even without pen and paper). The faculty knew that the SHeL seminar created a feeling of belonging and integration into the department, and helped them and their graduate students alike to stay up to date with each other's research. The question and answer (Q&A) session at the end of each talk was particularly useful in this regard. The seminar was a way of being socialized into the professional life of the department. Though I began to understand the importance of attending this kind of event, I felt uneasy about participating. The Q&A period at the end of the talk was especially uncomfortable for me. Everyone in the audience chimed in with comments for the speaker. It was intimidating because professors and graduate students asked the presenters questions I could not understand, much less comment on. Many questions pertained to the statistical methods results the presenters mentioned in their talks. And just to add to the fun, statistical jargon ran rampant throughout these discussions. Professors would ask things like: What is the distribution of your dependent variable? What are the standard errors for the coefficients you presented today? Were they relatively high or low? How does that impact your interpretation of the results? Did you test your model for multicollinearity? Did you run the VIF (variation inflation factor) test?

This statistical jargon was beyond my comprehension. I had not yet taken a graduate level statistics course, so when the professors made comments, they may as well have been speaking in a foreign language. I felt myself going into a type of mental shock where suddenly nothing made any sense to me at all. I bucked up, however, and forced myself to keep going to these torturous events, with the vague hope that someday the light would shine through the darkness.

During the first few workshop presentations I sat in the back of the room. I felt disconnected with the conversation because I barely knew enough about the topics to follow the talks, let alone ask an intelligent question at the end. There in my position of safety at the rear, I took what notes I could, and did my best to become invisible during the Q&A session. After the second SHeL session, I realized that none of the first-year graduate students had said a word during the Q&A period. I wondered what was going through their minds after the presentations. Were they as nervous as I was about making a comment at the end of the talks? Back at the lab that day, I asked them straight up: "What do you guys think about the SHeL seminar? Do you feel completely lost sometimes?"

Mark quickly jumped in and responded, "I think it's excellent, and even though I don't get everything, I feel like I'll learn more as we advance in the program. So, all in all, I like the workshops and I even had a few questions in mind during the last session. But I didn't ask them because we ran out of time."

Alison replied, "Well, I for one don't think I'll be attending anymore. It's just way over my head and I feel like it's not the best use of my time right now. I'll learn more later and then I might feel comfortable going in the future."

Ronald chimed in, "But this is what grad school is all about—higher-order thinking—and I'm ready for the challenge. I'm getting the gist of these presentations and I'm thinking I will be ready to present something next year!"

Ronald's attitude was a little intimidating. I wasn't very forthcoming about how I felt about the seminar, but I think I could most relate to Alison's perspective. I too felt like I was in way over my head. My trepidation at the workshops did not discourage me from being a regular audience member, however. I recognized that I was learning a lot just by listening to the interactions of the professors and more senior graduate students, even if I was unfamiliar with the content of the talks.

One of the main things I was learning had to do with the communication style that the speakers and audience engaged in. These sometimes intense exchanges between the audience and the speakers were hard to get used to. Although I knew that the professors and students were not necessarily attempting to sabotage the speakers, sometimes their questions were very sharp and almost critical. Then again, other times their inquiries were made in a very nonthreatening way. I kept wondering how the speakers could tolerate the feeling of vulnerability—they never knew what was going to come at them. After a few of these sessions it became clear to me that the audience was genuinely invested in offering constructive criticism to make the research better. In general the audience had a true intellectual curiosity about the topics the presenters covered, and once I started to see this, the Q&A sessions started to become interesting events, rather than forty minutes of confusion.

Then, during the third SHeL workshop, one of my first-year colleagues surprised our cohort by boldly asking a question after one of the presentations. In fact, it was Ronald. He asked about the research design of the project that had been presented. From my assessment, his question voiced an appropriate concern, and the presenter seemed to answer it with ease. Ronald was the first one to break the ice, so to speak, for us first-year grad students. Who would be next?

As the semester moved forward and I faithfully continued to attend the SHeL seminar every week, I made another interesting observation. I started to notice that one of the most esteemed faculty members asked questions often, and many times she addressed something that seemed quite obvious. Her questions were very straightforward and simple, and audience members were not put off when she asked them. Especially important is that the clarification that came from her pointed yet simple inquiries was very helpful for me and, quite likely, the rest of audience. This made me realize that sometimes it's okay to ask about basic issues and that it may be helpful for presenters to think critically about the main points they are trying to make.

Given this newfound insight, I was then determined to ask a question at one of the workshops, especially because by the middle of the semester most of the other first-year graduate students were raising their hands, making comments, and posing questions to the presenters. Everyone that is, except for me. I remained too shy to dive into the fray. Why couldn't I? I still had this nagging fear that I would ask something totally stupid and irrelevant, especially if I just made something up to sound good. So, I had to be sure that my comment was fully thought out and that it was worth saying before I just launched into it in front of all the professors and senior graduate students in the department. I also started to notice that people were going up to the presenters after the session to discuss issues that weren't covered during the Q&A. I figured that this approach might work for me. Then, near the end of the semester, at the end of one of these weekly presentations, a strange thing happened. There was a presentation on race relations in the United States, which was a research interest of mine. In fact, I had just read an article by a well-known sociologist, Eduardo Bonilla-Silva, whom the speaker referenced in her talk. I noticed myself feeling that I actually knew enough about this topic to formulate a very good question! I found myself taking a sincere intellectual interest in the talk I had just heard. Hmmm. Dare I raise my hand? Was it going to be a stupid comment or an intelligent contribution? I felt confident that I knew what I was asking, but I was still too timid to ask in front of everyone, so I approached the speaker when the session was over, and she welcomed my question. She said it was a good one and gave me a helpful answer.

After having a pretty positive response from the presenter, I crossed the threshold of my insecurity and became quite comfortable with asking my questions, but only in one-on-one conversations. I typically saved my comments for the end and posed them to the professors after their talks. In not too long a time, I gained confidence because none of the speakers ever seemed to think my inquiries were stupid or lacking foundation. Then one day my stage fright finally left me. I actually raised my hand at the end of the talk and asked my question in front of everyone. The presenter answered me with appreciation for my insight. I was stunned, but proud.

By the second year, I was able to participate in the SHeL colloquia with much more confidence. I no longer hid in the back of the room all the time. I often sat toward the front so I could clearly understand the presenters and more easily engage them in a fruitful dialog following their talks. I also began e-mailing my feedback to the presenters if I didn't have time to stay for the Q&A sessions.

In hindsight, I have realized that being in the uncomfortable place of *not knowing* was the first step in a process that led to the day I could feel comfortable with the material more advanced graduate students and faculty presented in these workshops. Moreover, it was essential for me to see examples of what is expected in an academic presentation. For instance, I learned that there is a standard procedural order for these events in my department. First comes the presentation followed by comments, and then Q&A. Rare is the occasion when speakers are interrupted mid-presentation by audience members. Also, presenters typically use PowerPoint, and their presentations include an introduction, a literature review, research questions, data and methods, findings, and a conclusion. Once familiar with the format, I knew what to expect and could more easily participate.

Thus, my attendance at those workshops taught me not only how to intelligently interact with professionals in my field, it showed me the steps needed for advanced academic presentations. The seminar was critical to my understanding of the structure of presentations for an academic audience. In addition, on a subtler level, I gained insight into the culture of my academic department, and how to place myself in it—for one day I would have to get up there and give a presentation myself, although this didn't happen until the fourth year of my graduate program. So, it was very helpful to learn in advance which professors would pose the most challenging questions, which presentations were well organized and which ones seemed to need more work, and which graduate students and faculty members were doing research in my sub-field. Furthermore, facing my fear eventually had another positive outcome: I gained more confidence in my ability to present my own research as I slowly but surely gleaned knowledge about my field of study, which of course was why I was there in the sociology program in the first place. Although it took an arduous effort, I did in the end become a very active member of the SHeL seminar and an effective academic presenter.

If I would have shied away from this challenge in the face of my insecurities, I think I might have had many difficulties down the line in my program. As a result of sticking with the seminar I knew what was expected for in-class presentations in the graduate courses I was taking, as well as the undergraduate courses I was teaching. In the end, I had established my brand as an intelligent and reliable contributor to the sociology department.

Christy's story is a good example of the type of fortitude it takes to assimilate into the culture of a graduate program during the first year. She overcame her inner fear and was able to maintain a positive attitude about herself and her goals as she learned to participate fully in her new academic environment.

Another type of challenge confronted Jamelle, who also tells about overcoming a difficult first-year experience. Like Christy, she did not let her unexpected situation defeat her. Jamelle's experience involved a crisis in her academic life. She found that when one door closed, another door opened, as described in her story. In the end she succeeded.

Staying True to Myself

Jamelle: In the late spring after I had graduated from Tuskegee University with my BA and before I started my first year of graduate school in chemistry, I participated in a summer research program at my new graduate institution, Purdue University. So, the process of establishing myself in the Department of Chemistry began a few months earlier for me than for most of my first-year colleagues. The purpose of the summer program is to help new graduate students acclimate and provide a head start on research. In chemistry, this head start also involves an initial selection of the new student's professor and lab group ("lab"), which will become the academic and research home base for the duration of the student's graduate program. After the initial selection of a lab, however, more interviews follow, and official departmental paper-work has to be processed—something like immigrating to a new country. To add to the stress, graduate students in my department are not guaranteed that they will actually get their first choice of professor and lab group. With regard to my story, making this choice turned out to be a little more difficult than I had anticipated.

What made it difficult? you might ask. Well, I'm a very straightforward person. Some people call me blunt; others call me outspoken and say I'm too direct. The way I see things, it is more important for people to know where they stand with me than for me to be superficially nice so that everyone likes me. Another thing about me: once I decide I like something, I tend to stick with it. These personality traits have caused me a problem or two in the past. Little did I realize that they might be an issue in graduate school. When I faced the reality of my strong personality, I felt enabled to successfully estab-lish my brand as a truthful PhD candidate of high integrity and, as you will see, it all worked out in the end.

When new graduate students in my department arrive on campus in the summer, they generally must rely on the university website to identify profes-sors who share their research interests. Many of the faculty members are away from campus during the summer months, and some don't return until the be-ginning of the fall semester. I, along with many of the other summer program participants, did not have an opportunity to engage in face-to-face interactions with many faculty members before making a lab choice. So, I chose my lab group out of a pure interest in the topic that group was researching. I admit, I didn't give too much consideration to group dynamics, but I didn't sense that there would be any problems. And, I liked the research topic of this group so much that I didn't see the need to check around to find out what other labs were doing. Some of the summer research program students moved around from one lab group to another to see which one they liked best, but I didn't feel the need to do this. So, I worked in Professor Hammond's research group all summer, although I had not met him in person yet.

During the summer I also made friends with Sarah, another first-year stu-dent who was participating in the summer research opportunity program. De-spite the fact that she and I had chosen different labs to work in that summer, we hit it off pretty quickly, and I was glad to have a friend in this new place so far from home. I often discussed with her my excitement at the possibility of continuing my graduate work in the lab I had chosen. The research topic covered in the lab intrigued me, and I felt that my skill set could contribute to the team of students in the lab. Among my lab colleagues, I freely expressed my thoughts and opinions about the decisions we were making each week. I acquired good research experience, and gleaned all that I could from my fellow lab members. That said, at the end of the summer research program, I believed that my interactions in this lab group had been very positive, and so I regarded it as the place I would call home throughout the course of my graduate studies. It did not work out that way, however.

At the beginning of the semester after classes were underway, I made an appointment with Dr. Hammond to discuss my interest in joining his lab group. He was very cordial and said he would be happy to take me on as one of his students in his lab, but as I already knew, this was just an informal agreement, ahead of the official decision, which involved signatures and paperwork later in the semester. Nevertheless, I felt very glad that he had initially accepted me, and that I had a lab that I knew I wanted to be part of my target academic home for the next five years.

After about two months the time drew near when we officially had to choose and be accepted by an advisor. Now came the time to fill out the specific departmental forms and get the signatures of the necessary parties involved. In a way these forms are much like a work contract, because the professor is agreeing to take you through the five years of research that will constitute the dissertation for your PhD. So, I went to see Dr. Hammond to see where things stood in terms of my position in his lab. At the time, I thought of this meeting as merely a formality, because it seemed to me that he and the lab group and I were a great fit. Still, I knew I had to see if his offer was still on the table. After a few minutes in his office, I could sense quite clearly that his attitude toward me had changed. He told me without much explanation that he didn't think it would work out for me to join his lab, and that I should go check with the other research groups for one to join.

Needless to say, I was devastated. The door that had seemed open had suddenly slammed shut. Words cannot describe the disappointment I felt on that day. I was even reconsidering whether I had made the right decision to attend the summer program. Perhaps if I had not attended it, I wouldn't have gotten my hopes up about joining this particular lab. I phoned my friend Sarah, and she was very supportive. She was shocked that I would not be able to join the lab because she, like me, was under the impression that I had done well there that summer. She asked me why I hadn't asked Dr. Hammond for more information about why he had changed his mind. In fact, I had not asked Dr. Hammond why he had made this decision. I guess I was just too shocked to ask him. My lackluster response to Dr. Hammond made me feel even worse. Despite Sarah's efforts to help, I still felt really alone because she couldn't really understand where I was coming from—she had secured her spot in a lab that worked for her. The really awful thing was that by this time it was too late to find another lab that had a free space. All of the other professors had already chosen the students they would take on in their labs. I had unwittingly put all of my eggs in one basket by not visiting other labs or interviewing with the other professors in the program over the summer and in the early fall. Suddenly I was an orphan in my department and had no place to call home.

Despite the gravity of my situation, I did not give up or take a victim stance and gossip about the group that had rejected me. And I tried not to discuss the professor either, although this was difficult, because at the time I was bitter, upset, and disappointed. I did think about quitting altogether, but this seemed like a really bad idea. I had worked so hard to get where I was, and after all, I was still a member of the chemistry department. I just needed to find a lab to call home. I did my best to stay positive and trust that somehow things would work out. I kept going to my classes and kept up with my studies. After a week or two of this horrible limbo, one day after one of my classes I met my friend Sarah for coffee. Oddly, she was excited. She said she had a little secret to tell me that no one else knew about. Sarah had heard that one of the people in her lab group had been approved to switch to cellular biology and as a result there would be a space in her lab next semester. She then suggested it might be possible for me to join her lab! The research area in Sarah's lab was related to what I had been doing, so maybe she had found an open door for me. With hope in my heart, I scheduled a meeting the next day with the professor who was in charge of Sarah's lab. I still recall that meeting.

As I walked to Dr. Epstein's office, I started to get a little anxious. My heart was beating faster than usual, and I felt a bead of sweat drip down my forehead. I could not believe that this was happening to me. I'm typically the person in control and not overtly affected by stress. But this decision was out of my hands and it made me feel powerless. I heard my footsteps on the shiny tiled floor as I approached Dr. Epstein's lab. I stopped and took a deep breath and tried to relax, and then went into the lab and saw Dr. Epstein sitting in her office at her desk. She welcomed me with a warm smile and a friendly handshake, and immediately I felt a lot more at ease. She asked me about my previous research experience, available work hours, and how my adjustment to Purdue had been so far. I knew that I was taking a risk by telling her the truth about my bad experience, but true to form, I was forthright and to the point about my experience with the first lab. She raised her eyebrows after hearing that I hadn't been accepted by them. She suggested that we go meet the rest of the graduate students in her lab.

I thought then that I was a goner. How would this new group take to having a new person at this stage of the game? I took a deep breath and dutifully followed Dr. Epstein around the corner to the cubicles where each student had a desk. Sarah was there, along with several other friendly looking people. Dr. Epstein introduced me to them. I smiled and said hello. She told them a little about my interests and that I would like to join the group. The people in the room looked at me with friendly faces and nodded as I started to talk in my unreserved style about my recent research projects. Several of them actually clicked with me and started asking me more about what I had been doing, and I asked them about their work as well. Pretty soon we were engaged in a great conversation—the students, Dr. Epstein, and I. After a few minutes, Dr. Epstein looked around at us and said, "Well, Jamelle, I think you will be fine here. Where is another desk?" Sarah showed me to a vacant desk in the lab, in between the lab's refrigerator and a big file cabinet. It was slightly cramped, but I didn't care. I left feeling extremely relieved and very grateful. Miracles are still possible. Dr. Epstein had decided to take me on! The door had opened on my academic home sweet home at last.

Although my new lab situation had worked out, I was still perplexed as to why Dr. Hammond had not taken me on as I thought he had promised he would. So, I decided to ask the members of his lab group, my first group of so-called friends, why I had been rejected. They told me that he did not accept me because the group had decided that my strong personality and outspoken nature would not be conducive to the group's dynamics. I was a little taken aback by this, but I found comfort in knowing that my rejection was not because of academic reasons. Although his sudden about-face had been upsetting at first, I realized later that being myself had spared me from spending five years with a group of people who did not accept or appreciate me for who I am. The group had done the right thing by being honest about their preferences, and I had done the right thing by being myself, even though it had caused me some upset.

At the end of the day, I am very glad I did not end up in that lab group. Although I have learned to temper my outspoken style over the years of my graduate career, I have remained true to myself, and doing this early on was extremely important to establishing my brand of honesty and sincerity in my department and among my colleagues, and most importantly, for my own sense of self and my self-esteem.

——→

Jamelle's story is a reminder of two old adages: *To thine own self be true* and *Patience is the mother of virtue*. She believed in herself when the going got rough and then had the strength to wait for another opportunity to present itself. She didn't escalate the problem with gossip and, in the end, Jamelle was able to overcome rejection, still finding her place in her department without sacrificing her integrity.

Another situation that requires adjustment for new graduate students involves interpersonal communication and sharing research ideas with colleagues. Lauren was in a lab where she witnessed her first-year colleague Amelia go through a professional interaction in which she felt betrayed, yet she too was able to rise above these difficulties and go on to successfully establish her brand of reliability and social integrity in her department. Amelia's situation challenged her professionalism, but she met the problem squarely and in the end had a stronger footing in her department and with herself, as Lauren describes in the following story.

Speaking Up Just Enough

Lauren: Graduate school, and academia as a whole, can be very competitive, and learning to manage one's work amid this competition is very important. The competition can involve grades, the favor of professors and, most importantly, ideas and content for research projects. Graduate students can be made and broken by the originality of their ideas and research designs. I learned about this when I watched Amelia, a first-year grad student lab colleague, go through a tough learning experience involving her research ideas. During the summer before I began my graduate program, a senior graduate student in my department, Jack, was working in our lab as a mentor. He introduced Amelia and others into our lab group. Because Jack was a senior graduate student and seemed reliable, Amelia felt comfortable sharing with him her research ideas and the variables that she wanted to use for her research project from the data set she was developing.

Then one day Amelia needed help with some fine points in her data set, and so she consulted Jack about her variables. He seemed very interested in what she was doing, but instead of helping her with her questions, Jack unexpectedly discouraged Amelia from using her data set, saying that our lab advisor, Dr. Bentley, hadn't approved those variables. So the next day Amelia asked Dr. Bentley about the variables and he indeed discouraged her from using them for her first project, suggested some alternatives, and also said that she could think about using them later in her graduate studies. Although she didn't fully understand their reasoning, she trusted Jack and Dr. Bentley because they were more experienced in this field. She decided to follow their suggestions, and later told Jack about what Dr. Bentley had said. Jack was glad that Dr. Bentley had agreed with him, and advised Amelia to continue with the research project that Dr. Bentley thought was more suitable for her.

A few weeks later Amelia was having some issues trying to navigate the new data set she had started working with, and Dr. Bentley told her to talk to Jack because he was knowledgeable about it and could better assist her. So Amelia again asked Jack for feedback. While helping her navigate her data set, Jack opened up one of his files to show her an example to address the problems that she was having. When he opened his file, Amelia noticed that many of the variables that he had were very similar to the ones that earlier she had proposed to use. So, she asked Jack why he had those variables in his files. He responded, "Don't you remember, I've been working on a paper with these variables? We discussed it last month." Amelia was certain he had never talked about these data before seeing her working with them. She told us about Jack's comments and none of us in the lab had heard anything about this project of his. Amelia knew she had not discussed it with him or us. From then on, we were suspicious that he was using her variables for his own work, and Amelia became wary of talking with him about her research and other ideas that she had. Actually, we all became careful about telling Jack about our projects.

At that point Amelia didn't know what to do. She could have talked about it with everyone, including her friends and family, and gossiped about him to the other graduate students, but she didn't. She felt that such behavior would reflect badly on her and wouldn't help the situation, although she did confide in me about it, and I agreed that she should be careful how she dealt with this situation.

Then her worst suspicions became reality. The following year, Jack published an article based on the variables that he had learned about from Amelia's research. She was hurt because she had trusted him with her research ideas, and he had betrayed her. Again, she could have gossiped about this with people in the department, but she didn't. She knew she needed to confront Jack, to gain a sense of peace about the situation. It took her several weeks, but she finally got up the courage to talk with him about his use of the variables in his publication. She told him she felt he had secretly used her research ideas, and she felt hurt by this. He said that it was not like that, but didn't have a real concrete reason as to why. He was not forthcoming with any further response, so Amelia simply said that he needed to be careful in the future about what he did with other people's research, even someone in their first year. She felt glad that she had confronted him, and that she hadn't just let his actions go by unnoticed.

The next day when she was in the lab, she saw Dr. Bentley and went over to his desk to ask him about the upcoming lab meeting. He was very cool toward her and said he wasn't sure about the time of the meeting and that he didn't have time to talk. This type of behavior for some professors might have been normal, but for Dr. Bentley, who was known for his gregarious and friendly personality, it was very strange. Amelia put two and two together and figured that Jack had talked with Dr. Bentley about her conversation with him the day before. At that point, she felt even more betrayed because not only had Jack possibly used her research ideas, he might also have shared their private conversation with her major advisor.

Now Amelia felt like she had a very serious problem on her hands. It was one thing to be on bad terms with a senior graduate student, but another situation altogether to be on bad terms with the lab's major advisor. Jack would be graduating in the spring—she might never see him again. But Dr. Bentley and she would be working together for another four and a half years. What if he decided that she was a difficult student with whom he didn't want to work? Very upset, Amelia came to talk with me about the situation. I asked her if she was sure that Jack had talked with Dr. Bentley. Maybe he had something else on his mind when she went to ask him about the lab meeting. I cautioned her about drawing conclusions when she couldn't really be sure about them. Amelia seemed relieved that the possibility could exist that Jack hadn't told Dr. Bentley about his conversation with her. But what about the original situation, where Dr. Bentley had dissuaded her from using the data set that Jack had told him about? Whom could she trust? I didn't have much to offer in the way of solutions for her there. Dr. Bentley's advice not to use that data set, and then Jack's use of it for his article, did not bode well for Amelia's trust in Dr. Bentley.

Accusing a senior colleague of using your research ideas is a serious action, but even worse would be casting aspersions on your major professor. Amelia didn't feel at that time that she was in the position as a junior graduate student to formally make this charge. Looking back on it, she said that she was glad that she hadn't gossiped about the situation and escalated the problem, yet she also felt good that she did at least confront Jack so that she didn't feel like she had let him completely get away with what seemed to be dishonest behavior. From this experience, she learned to play her cards closely and to be careful with whom she chose to share her work. But most of all, she learned to preserve her professional brand in her department as someone who is careful, smart, and sticks up for herself in appropriate ways.

Amelia switched lab groups in the end. Her professional interests shifted, so when she completed her master's degree she changed departments. The second time around she researched carefully whom she wanted as her advisor and made a choice that was a much better fit for her. I was greatly relieved to see her make this change and to successfully complete her program. Many students would have given up under similar circumstances, but she stuck with it, established her brand as a high-integrity graduate student, and achieved her goals in the end.

As Christy, Jamelle, and Lauren relate, the graduate school environment requires a mature and self-confident yet tactful approach to teamwork. Establishing their brand, or learning the limitations of the graduate school environment without compromising their own integrity, gave them a foothold from which they could pursue their graduate studies as people of commitment, responsibility, and achievement. These lessons form a significant number of the hurdles new graduate students need to learn to navigate. Other sets of challenges stand ready to test the first-year student, however, as the following narrative describes.

THE INVISIBLE HAZARD: SOCIAL ISOLATION

Anyone who has a very busy job knows the hazards of social isolation. Graduate school can be particularly challenging in this regard. Preparing for graduate courses, conducting thesis research, planning for teaching courses, and grading student papers can lead to the inadvertent exclusion of friends and family from a graduate student's calendar. Another way that graduate students can become socially isolated is by being fully funded and not needing to teach in order to afford their graduate education.

Christy relates the hurdles she faced as a lucky graduate student with full funding from a major funding agency. Not connected to a lab and free to work full time on her coursework and research, she encountered another problem—that of professional and social isolation. Her story tells about how she struggled with and then solved her dilemma by reaching out to her department and university for support, which helped her make it through her first year of graduate school.

Surviving My Good Fortune

Christy: At the end of my senior year of college in Houston, Texas, I was very excited to be graduating and obtaining my bachelor's degree. It had been a challenging journey, but I had a fulfilling sense of accomplishment knowing that I had successfully completed my degree and that I was now taking on the challenge of acquiring two advanced degrees in graduate school. So during the spring of my senior year I was on an academic high. Having been accepted into a few graduate programs and recruited by some of the strongest doctoral programs in the country, I was feeling great. After giving it much consideration, I decided to attend Indiana University (IU). A few weeks later, I was notified that I had received the fellowship I had applied for a few months earlier. So, I would be entering the IU master's program in sociology with three years of funding from a predoctoral fellowship from the Ford Foundation Fellowship Program.

After receiving my BA, I felt totally right with the world because I was funded to attend the graduate program of my choice. Several people expressed concern about my decision to attend graduate school in Indiana, however. One of my faculty advisors was worried about the lack of racial and ethnic diversity in Bloomington and wanted me to consider attending a graduate program in a larger city, or at least in a more diverse area of the country. My parents and my sister, with whom I have a very close relationship, were surprised that I didn't select some of the other schools on my list since they sounded more prestigious. I tried to explain to them that the strengths of my particular graduate program were more important than the overall prestige of the university and that having someone (or several people) in the role of an academic advisor with whom I really wanted to work was one of the most important factors in my decision to attend IU. My family was also on edge about my moving so far away from home. I had spent most of my life in Texas. Despite all their concerns, my family was very supportive of my decision and did everything they could to help make my transition from undergrad to graduate school as smooth as possible.

Graduate school at IU started in late August. When I arrived in Bloomington in mid-August, the graduate student who had hosted me during my visit to Indiana in the spring picked me up from the airport and drove me to the apartment I had rented for the year. She was very helpful, and I was impressed with her willingness to go out of her way for someone she didn't know that well. It was great to already have at least one dependable person in my life in Bloomington. Over the next week or so, I settled into my new apartment and got better acquainted with the city. Given that I had received external funding, I did not need to work as a teaching assistant (TA) or take a job as a research assistant (RA) for a faculty member. My only assignment was to do well in my coursework, and this didn't start for another week. Thus, my first week in Bloomington felt more like a break from work than the beginning of an extremely rigorous graduate program.

When classes started, things got back to normal and I was busy again, but not like my classmates with teaching and research assistantships. While in theory the freedom I had sounds like it would be a great way to adjust to life as a graduate student, in fact, just doing coursework all on my own all of the time made for a lonely and isolating existence. My parents' and family's concerns started to register with me in a painful way. Consider my circumstances: I had relocated to Indiana for grad school from Texas, where I had lived my entire life. Back in my family home in Dallas, I had always been surrounded by my parents, grandparents, uncle, aunts, and a host of cousins. As a result of being so far away from them, I felt really disconnected from the people I was closest to. Also, my move to Indiana was the first time I had ever lived on my own without a roommate. Despite the many graduate student orientations and get-togethers, by the end of the first few weeks after my arrival in Bloomington, the excitement of the move had dissipated.

It started to sink in that I had relocated from a cosmopolitan, multicultural environment to the more or less monotone culture of the Midwest: from

Houston, Texas, to Bloomington, Indiana. These two cities are very different from each other in terms of their racial/ethnic composition. One-quarter of the residents in Houston are African American, while only one person in twenty-five identifies as being African American in Bloomington. Despite the fact that my undergraduate institution was predominantly white, Houston's big-city environment offered many culturally diverse events and activities. As for Bloomington, I was impressed by the inviting town square area, its little specialty boutiques and stores, and its inviting variety of restaurants. Although Bloomington initially seemed to be a generally friendly place, after a few months I felt stifled because I saw significantly fewer people who looked like me (i.e., racial/ethnic minorities) walking on the streets of this quaint Midwestern town.

Although things actually started out okay with my move to IU and all of the social events welcoming new graduate students, these events occurred much less frequently after the first three weeks or so. Once the semester was in full swing, social events in general quickly tapered off, and the new friends I had made at these events disappeared into the overwhelm of their responsibilities as graduate TAs or RAs. And, all of my graduate student colleagues, the people I met in my classes with whom I could have spent some social time, also had teaching or research assistantships and did not have much free time for socializing. I, on the other hand, had the opportunity to focus fully on my coursework. Unfortunately this opportunity soon became as much of a problem as it was a blessing. When I wasn't in class, I was alone all the time. No study buddies had time to join me at the library. I attempted studying in different locations on and off campus to add some variety to my schedule. One time, I walked over to the campus coffee shop to study, and after reading for a while, I looked around me and realized that I was the only visible minority in the place. Although no one was being impolite to me, I felt invisible. No one paid attention to me. No one said hello. No one smiled at me. Since people seemed to be so focused on doing their own thing, I became more reserved and my typically friendly demeanor changed into a type of bland indifference.

I came to learn that students with fellowships are not in the majority in graduate programs. In the eyes of my colleagues with assistantships, I was living the good life since I had the luxury of a prestigious fellowship and could focus fully on my coursework and eventual research. Consequently, I did not want to lament my loneliness to my first-year TA friends. Little did they know that I was feeling so unfulfilled and very lonely. Moreover, although the introductory classes I was taking were generally very interesting, I often felt that they were not directly addressing my research interests at the time. (This is the nature of most graduate programs. In retrospect, I can see that these classes were providing a foundation for my general knowledge of sociology; in fact, once I got to more advanced courses that were specific to my research area [e.g., medical sociology], I realized that I most certainly needed the foundational knowledge. This time was lonely, but it was extremely important to my later success.) So there I was, diligently going to class and writing papers, but growing more and more uninspired because of social isolation. I ate many meals alone and attended several events by myself that first semester. At first it felt weird to go out by myself, but I adjusted to doing things on my own because I knew very well that my new friends in Bloomington were usually too busy to hang out and go to concerts and movies.

I remember the first event I attended alone. It was a show called *Potpourri of the Arts* at a popular theater in downtown Bloomington on a Friday night. Instead of even attempting to ask someone to go along with me, I went ahead and purchased a single ticket in advance. I really enjoyed the show and was amazed at the talent of the students who were in it. But, I couldn't shake the thought that I could be doing this kind of thing all the time with close friends and family if only I was back in Texas. Oh the frustration. It put a serious damper on my mood. The show lasted about two hours, and afterward I wanted to go grab a bite to eat. I really wanted to go to one of those enticing restaurants downtown, but not alone. So I decided to stop by the fast-food place near my apartment instead. I went to bed early that night and probably shed a tear or two.

Fortunately, I did have a close friend from my undergrad years in Houston who dried my tears with me over the phone. I talked with her regularly and she was very supportive. She was definitely my major confidant during this difficult time. It was great having her listening ear, someone I could really talk to. But, it also made me a little sad. I so desperately wanted to be close to the things, people, and places that were familiar to me, but of course this was impossible.

I was beginning to seriously reconsider my decision to move to Bloomington. During my first semester at IU, I had dozens of long phone conversations with my friend in Houston about whether or not I would stay there. In those talks I often contemplated leaving the program, with the idea that

I would go back to Houston to find a graduate program at home. Over time I spoke with my family less often, and I even started to consider quitting graduate school altogether. I did not tell my family though, because I didn't want to disappoint them, and I didn't want them to be too worried about me. Leaving my graduate program just didn't sit right with me, however. I didn't want to be a quitter. Giving up on all that I had worked so hard to achieve seemed counterproductive to my professional goals and to me as a person. My brand was about making things work, despite my misery, and so I never actually decided to leave.

Instead I stayed, and looking back on it I believe I did this because a few very bright spots were slowly emerging onto the dark field of my isolated horizon. First, the professor of the social psychology course I took in my first semester turned out to be absolutely excellent. I knew I could work with her and that she would eventually become my main advisor. Throughout the course, I would visit her during office hours when I didn't understand the readings or was having difficulty in the class. She was very helpful, and she challenged me to think like a sociologist. The course gave me the opportunity to get to know her teaching style, mentoring style, and personality. The interactions I had with her during this first semester were crucial to establishing a positive mentoring relationship from the very beginning of my academic work. Her class was very challenging, but I learned a lot, grew more confident, and had the opportunity to start laying the groundwork for a mentor-mentee relationship with her as a faculty member in my department.

The other bright spot came when I decided to search out campus activities that I had enjoyed as an undergrad: I got the idea to try to re-create the life I had back in Houston in order to mitigate the isolation I was experiencing. I didn't really know whether this would work, but I figured it was worth a shot, even though things were picking up with my classes and I was frequently inundated with my graduate coursework. One week, for example, I had something major due for each class. I had to turn in a take-home test for Social Theory, write a draft of a literature review due for Research Methods, and put together a short presentation for my Social Psychology course, all in the same week. Despite these demands, I remembered how I had been very involved in a gospel choir back in Houston.

A few minutes on the web and my search led me to the IU gospel choir's web page. Though it appeared to be a mostly undergraduate group, I decided that I would attend the first meeting to see what it was like. Originally, I thought I might feel completely out of place and awkward. However, when I walked into their first rehearsal, many smiling and inviting faces welcomed me into their circle. I felt at home right away. And, they sang many tunes I used to sing with my gospel choir from college. The other thing I really liked was that the group met only two hours a week and had a singing event no more than once a month, which was a manageable commitment for my schedule. I sang with this group throughout my first year of graduate school and it did a lot to fill the void in my social life.

I had also enjoyed being a member of the Black Student Association during my Houston undergraduate years, so I was elated to discover that IU had a Black Graduate Student Association (BGSA). I still recall attending the first meeting where the sight of over fifty African American graduate students in one room totally amazed me. I was simultaneously shocked and pleased to be among such vibrant, gifted black graduate students. My racial background has always been an important part of my self-identity, and it was very reassuring to me to know that IU had this large network of students with whom I shared common roots. This group of students refreshed my sense of identity and at the same time empathized with my concerns around the racial climate of my department. They also provided practical advice on ways to cope with insecurities related to issues of racial identity and academic achievement. Though I didn't actually re-create my undergraduate years (thank goodness!), I feel that my participation in these organizations and my new friendships allowed me to begin to appreciate the good things my graduate program and the city of Bloomington had to offer.

In addition, I also reached out to graduate students with whom I shared a similar academic background and established friendships with a few advanced students in my own department. Since they were working on their dissertations, their time was more flexible than that of the TAs with teaching responsibilities. These senior grad students provided a supportive environment where I could express my frustrations, and they gave me advice about how to navigate the doctoral program. Without their support, I don't think I would have continued, so I am still extremely grateful for their concern and willingness to spend countless hours listening to my graduate school woes. Eventually I rose above my difficulties and became one of the people who commiserated supportively with the new grad students in order to help them adjust to the intense demands of graduate student life. I started to feel that there was a place for me in this completely new setting after all.

Though it has been a long process, one that has often felt like an uphill journey, I am currently quite satisfied with my graduate program and I enjoy what the city of Bloomington has to offer in the way of cultural events. My perspective has changed. I originally felt like my life was "on hold" until I graduated with my PhD in hand. But, then I realized that it was important for me to actively combat isolation and to attend to both the academic and personal components of my life. That doesn't mean that I'm never discouraged, bored, or frustrated, or that I don't miss my family and friends in Houston, but it has been absolutely invaluable to be a part of academic and social communities during my years as a graduate student living away from my hometown.

Now I look back on the hours I spent talking with my friend in Houston. I was always available to talk whenever she called. Now when she calls, I'm usually busy with work or out with my friends, so I have to call her back. In retrospect, my experience of isolation, although difficult, taught me to be more independent, and to learn to do things on my own. This experience also showed me that it's okay to reach out to others and ask for help when I need it. And now as an advanced graduate student, I'm in the process of writing several research papers, working on my dissertation, and teaching undergraduate classes. I look back now and appreciate the more flexible schedule I had back in my first few years of graduate school. My fellowship allowed me to make an important transition—this being from my undergraduate studies into my graduate student life, and ultimately, my profession as a sociologist.

BALANCING TEACHING AND COURSEWORK

As Christy's narrative made clear, most graduate students work during their program as an RA or a TA for a professor who needs help with a research project or teaching undergraduate classes. These positions are paid by the graduate student's department and can be invaluable in providing financial support for graduate school. Furthermore, the department typically covers its graduate students' tuition. The danger with research assistantships and teaching responsibilities while pursuing a graduate degree, however, is that these assignments can make it difficult to complete the coursework required for the degree. Adequate time to do research and write the dissertation often evaporates in the face of a full teaching schedule. Effective prioritization and time management are essential while working as a lab assistant or a graduate teaching assistant. It is important to note, however, that despite the demands of the TA or RA assignment, the hands-on teaching and/or lab experience can greatly increase a student's chances of getting a job when the PhD is completed. Thus the incentive to work as a TA or an RA while in graduate school is very high.

The stories which follow provide a window into the challenges of balancing undergraduate teaching or lab assistance with graduate coursework while completing a graduate degree. Lauren and Sean tell about situations in which they watched two of their graduate student colleagues deal with the intense time management challenges. They were challenged to keep up with their coursework while teaching undergraduates and enduring circumstances which that demanded much fortitude and willpower. As a result, however, they learned to set limits according to their priorities so that they could make their teaching assistantships work for them and at the same time maintain their high standard of performance in their academic coursework. Lauren begins with her story about Marcelle, who learned a difficult lesson as she took on the responsibilities of a graduate TA position during her first semester as a graduate student.

Less Is More

Lauren: In the fall of my first year, I got to know my friend Marcelle, who had a half-time teaching assistantship for Sociology 101 during the first semester of her PhD program. Since the class was so big—five hundred students—she was hired as part of a group of eight TAs who took on the tasks of preparing the lecture room in advance of the class and handling administrative tasks, such as grading papers and answering student e-mails. The professor responsible for teaching the class planned and gave the lectures, which Marcelle also had to attend. Her official title was TA, and her job description required her to work twenty hours a week. That semester, however, her major advisor, Dr. Sinclair, also wanted her to write an application for a fellowship and to start research for her doctoral thesis. In addition, she had to take three required graduate courses in her field of sociology. These responsibilities put a major amount of work on her plate and she struggled with determining her priorities and knowing what needed to come first on her daily to-do list. She was not used to treating school as a job. Teaching had always been something important she knew she would have to do, but going to work as a TA every day was more demanding than she had expected. Hence, she did not know which of her jobs—being a teacher or being a student—needed her focus the most.

The class for which she was a TA was one of the more difficult classes to work with. Despite having more than five hundred students, the professor wanted everyone in the class to write what seemed like a vast amount of essays. Essay assignments take a great deal of time to grade, as compared with multiple choice tests with scan sheets that can be graded electronically. Even though several TAs shared the grading of the essays for this class, the workload was very challenging. It took enormous amounts of time—much beyond the twenty hours a week Marcelle was supposed to give to it. She often wondered why the department would give this job to a first-year graduate student who had never before been a TA. But such TA assignments for first-year graduate students are the norm. And not only are they the norm, they are much sought after by graduate students because having a TA or RA assignment means your tuition for your graduate courses is paid by the department. So many graduate students, Marcelle included, become part of the graduate TA workforce that does the grading (and sometimes the teaching) for undergraduate courses required for freshmen and sophomores.

Since Marcelle was being paid to teach and grade for this course, she often talked about how she related to her work as her *job*, and that she took it very seriously. She put her grading ahead of everything in order to make all the deadlines for the professor's course syllabus. She put the majority of her focus into it. Her reading for her graduate program courses was second on her to-do list. Consequently, she did not share her time equally with her homework for the classes she was taking as a graduate student. She knew she was giving this class more than the designated twenty hours required, and worried about the consequences of this imbalance. She struggled with knowing what needed to come first.

Then as she was leaving Dr. Sinclair's office one afternoon, I happened to see her and she told me that he had started to pressure her to complete the research proposal for the fellowship he had in mind for her. He said he would like to have a draft of this proposal by Thanksgiving. "Thanksgiving? How can I manage that?" Marcelle said, while reiterating that she was happy he thought she was good enough to try for this fellowship. Although she wondered how she could manage to draft the proposal and get all her work done for her TA job, Marcelle said she just obediently shook her head when Dr. Sinclair asked about it and told him that she would have it done by the deadline. She had wondered if he remembered that she had the Sociology 101 TA assignment, but she didn't want to bring it up. She didn't think she should tell him exactly what was going on with the TA job because she didn't want to sound like she was making excuses regarding the work it would take to put together the fellowship proposal. I suggested that she needed to tell him about her overload, but she thought it would be better just to try to meet the deadline and keep up with the TA responsibilities. Marcelle was overextended and she wasn't admitting it to herself.

She started to realize that her own coursework was really suffering through all of this. She was barely skimming the readings and, although she attended all of her classes and took copious notes, she was not putting enough time and effort into her homework assignments outside of class. In mid-October, like the five hundred freshmen in her TA class, Marcelle had a major midterm exam in a class we both were taking. After the exam Marcelle said to me, "I feel like I just slid into a brick wall." Later when we got our grades she confided in me, saying that she was devastated because she hadn't gotten her usual "A" on this test and wondered what was happening to her. She had worked herself to the bone to keep her undergraduate GPA at a 3.5 so that she could get into graduate school, and now here she was getting low grades. Nevertheless, she kept saying that she was doing the responsible thing by putting so much time into her grading—her job came first because the university was paying her. On top of this, she wasn't getting anything done on the fellowship proposal for her advisor. When I saw her not long before the Thanksgiving break, she was very distraught and had started questioning whether graduate school life was for her.

Fortunately, over the break she took the time to reflect on her experiences with me and a couple of our more senior graduate student colleagues, Lisa and Alex, who were in the third and fourth year of their programs. Of course none of us was going home for Thanksgiving. We were all buried under work that had to get done before the end of the semester. We went for coffee one morning before we hit the books and we all noticed that Marcelle was more than a little down. When she told us she regularly had been going over twenty hours each week with her TA job and was behind on everything and was thinking about quitting, Alex and Lisa scolded her and said, "No matter what, you cannot take time away from your coursework!" I had been telling her the same thing. She knew we were right. She told us about the proposal for her advisor and they suggested that she make an outline for it, just a very basic one, and to go talk with him as planned—even if the outline wasn't exactly what he would be expecting. Having it would be better than showing up empty-handed. They also made her swear that she would make the effort to organize her time and that she would take a time management seminar in January. Most of all, they forbade her from quitting after only one semester of graduate school, saying that they both had gone through similar scenarios, and told her, "You just have to set your priorities, make a schedule, and stick to it as best you can. If you fall down, pick yourself up, dust yourself off, and keep at it."

And so Marcelle was initiated into the graduate TAs school of hard knocks. In her second semester she did not make the same mistakes. She made a master schedule with all the assignment due dates and exams for her own classes and the grading deadlines for her TA job for the whole semester. Most importantly, she made sure that she adequately, and strictly, shared her time between her coursework and her teaching assistantship. She allotted the twenty hours, and only twenty hours, for her TA job, and put much more time into her coursework than she had done in the fall. Her customary grade of "A" returned to her exams and her papers. She had learned the hard way that her own studies had to come before her teaching, since her courses were teaching her the content she needed to learn as a new scholar in her field. Her coursework was the primary reason she was attending graduate school in the first place.

Although Marcelle had to go through the difficult experience of watching her grades suffer, with the support of her friends, she persevered and tried again—so the second time around she was wiser in the allocation of her time. Marcelle's story shows how important it is to plan your semester carefully in advance to keep from becoming overextended. She learned to set her limits and follow a schedule for her study time and was able to succeed in the end.

→

Yet another pitfall can trouble first-year TAs. In a story a little different from Lauren's about Marcelle, Sean tells about one of his first-year graduate student colleagues, Brendan, who learned the hard way that as a graduate TA, he had to keep a professional distance from his students in order for them to do their best in his class.

The Virtue of Tactful Limits

Sean: During my third year of grad school in mathematics, Brendan, one of the new graduate students in the math PhD program, had been assigned a sophomore calculus recitation section, Calculus 120, his first TA-ship. As Lauren also described, many graduate students receive their first-ever teaching assistantship in their first year of graduate school, which in math departments often involves teaching the recitation sessions for one section of a freshman or sophomore level class. In math departments a recitation section is typically a review session held twice a week in tandem with the course lectures given by the professor of the course. In this case, the professor was Dr. Harper and Brendan was the TA. The TA in the recitation section reviews the content of the lecture, explains homework questions, and proctors the weekly quizzes.

Calculus 120 covered calculus concepts in two dimensions and higher. This material is pretty challenging stuff for undergraduates, and graduate TAs usually command a good degree of respect from the freshmen they are teaching. Brendan, however, had been in an accelerated program in high school and skipped a year, so he was younger than the average graduate student. He would have been taken for being younger than he actually was anyway, even if he hadn't skipped a grade, because of his smaller stature and lack of a beard. As a result of looking so young, he got into some difficulties with his teaching.

In the second semester of his first year of graduate school, Brendan was very glad to have received a teaching assistantship. He wanted to be an instructor that his students could relate well with, one whom they trusted and knew was there for them as new freshmen on campus. So Brendan wanted to keep a relaxed atmosphere in his classroom. Instead of standing in front of the class all the time, he would work with his students at their tables during the recitation sessions. Brendan wanted to relate to his students as if he was a part of their crowd. And, he had them call him Brendan instead of Mr. Benitez. With his youthful appearance, his students tended to relate to him as a fellow student, instead of a teacher. Brendan discovered, however, that he had a hard time working with students who were so close to his own age. Working with them was stressful. Brendan complained to me more and more frequently that most of his students treated him like a buddy instead of their instructor. I know this is true because Brendan's office cubicle was adjacent to mine, and since they all liked Brendan so much, his students often came to his designated office hours to get extra individual help. They called him by his first name and joked with him like he was family. Even though I warned him not to do it, Brendan would often stay long past the end of his office hours to help his students.

Then one day I heard a very painful moan come from Brendan's cubicle. I went around the corner to see what was going on. He told me that the day before, when it was about six o'clock at the end of the school day, his student Barry, whom he had just been helping, asked him if he wanted to go for pizza and a beer. Brendan said, "Sure—why not?" He was really hungry and it was dinner time. So off he went with Barry. According to Brendan, while at the pizza place several other students from the class came in and were elated to see Brendan there with Barry. Everyone was having a great time talking and sharing stories, and before Brendan realized it, two hours had slipped by. He looked at his phone and panicked. Where did the time go? He had a major assignment due in his advanced mathematics theory seminar the next morning. He hurriedly gave his regrets to his students and rushed out to get home to do his assignment.

The next morning Brendan woke up exhausted because he had been up most of the night finishing his homework. He forced himself out of bed to make it to the seminar, homework assignment in hand. After lunch he went to the math office to pick up the new batch of quizzes for Calculus 120, which the students had just completed that morning. He rolled his eyes as he told me that one after the other they were coming up with near-failing or failing grades—all the students who had been at the pizza place with him the night before. I saw the stack of quizzes on his desk, loaded with red ink. He said he would now have to take a day from the class schedule to go over the quizzes and the information that they were supposed to know already. Not good. The night out for pizza had taken the place of their study time. Brendan felt like he was the cause of their failing grades.

He again talked to me about the buddy problem he was having. I told him, "You have to change your teaching style now, or your students will bury you." He said he knew that he needed to change, but wasn't sure exactly what to do. He had never learned how to be a graduate TA. I understood his situation and recommended that he go see Dr. Harper for some advice. This idea seemed okay to Brendan, but he was worried that he would look bad if he told Dr. Harper his problem. "Well, I wouldn't bring up the bit about going for pizza, but the age thing isn't your fault. Tell him that you need some tips about establishing your authority in the class. He is a very experienced professor and might have some practical advice for you," I said. The next time I saw Brendan, he was in better spirits. He said his professor was sympathetic, but he told Brendan, "You have to establish a professional boundary between you and your students. This doesn't mean that you are not their friend, it just means that you are their instructor first, and friend second."

Dr. Harper advised Brendan to adhere strictly to his office hours, just as I had suggested. He also suggested that Brendan use a sign-up sheet for his office hours, so that everyone would get a fifteen-minute time slot. This way they would know they were taking someone else's time if they stayed too long, and it would be easier for Brendan to end each session. Dr. Harper also advised him to remain at the front of the class while he was teaching and not sit down at the tables with the students. Brendan said these practical changes had already helped a lot. As far as the students' calling him Brendan, well he couldn't change that now, but Dr. Harper recommended that he use Mr. Benitez starting with the next semester's class. "And obviously," Brendan added, "I won't go out for pizza with them unless it's after the last quiz of the semester."

Sean's and Lauren's stories about Brendan's and Marcelle's first teaching experiences are good examples of how first-year graduate students can become overwhelmed by their new role as a TA. With the support of her graduate student colleagues, Marcelle was able to regroup with better self-discipline and time management in her following semester. Brendan had the presence of mind to go to his professor for advice, and he helped Brendan with strategies to overcome his challenge of being close in age to his students. Both Marcelle and Brendan made use of their available resources and learned valuable lessons, which helped each of them become a better TA and also a more successful graduate student.

THE PRIMARY CHALLENGE: QUALIFYING EXAMS

Although adjusting to work in a lab setting and balancing teaching with coursework are significant demands during the first year, the major challenge and preoccupation of the first two years of graduate school for most students is passing the doctoral or graduate exams. Crossing this threshold means that the graduate student has qualified, or has been given the go ahead, to research and write the dissertation. The pressure to pass one's graduate exams is the primary source of stress in the first two years of graduate school and is the underlying motivation for grad students to endure all of the other stresses of coursework and teaching.

Departments vary in the term they use for their graduate exams. They can be called qualifying exams, cumulative exams, comprehensive exams, or preliminary exams, depending on the department and field of study. And each of these terms has its own nickname: quals (qualifying), cumes (cumulative), comps (comprehensive), and prelims (preliminary). The reason for all the stress they cause is that a student's tenure in the graduate program can be terminated if these exams are not passed.

Graduate exams are often written exams, which test the student's basic or fundamental knowledge of her or his field. They are considered to be the first big hurdle in a graduate student's course of study, the first major rite of passage that students must make in order to reach the PhD. In certain departments, graduate students are allowed only a limited number of times to take the exam for each subject. Other departments allow up to two years to take and to pass these exams, with an unlimited amount of tries.

In the narratives that follow, Sean and Jamelle tell of their encounters and subsequent reengagements with their graduate exams. Both of them had to face this challenge more than once, and each has a story to tell about contending with this academic threshold and how it affected them. Sean relates how his experience with studying for, taking, and passing his qualifying exams was difficult, but as he describes, the process and its outcome was very much worth the effort.

A Positive Statistic

Sean: When I started my PhD program, I came to a rude awakening as to what being a graduate student was really like. On the one hand graduate school seemed to be about being smart, but after a while I learned that it was really about a heavy schedule, hard work, and determination. Most of all I learned that graduate school is about positive effort, especially when it comes to the qualifying exams.

In addition to keeping up with my program's coursework during the first year of my graduate program, I (along with all my classmates) also had to deal with taking and passing the qualifying exams or "quals," as math students often call them. These two quals are very important to graduate students in mathematics because everyone has to pass them in order to continue in the program. Qualifying exams in my department are based on the main topics in the field. Everyone studies very hard for these for obvious reasons.

Despite my best study efforts, however, I barely passed the first qualifier I took because, as I realized afterward, I had studied by myself. I learned that preparing for this challenge was too much for me alone, and several of my graduate student colleagues who had studied alone and also not done so well felt the same way. So a group of us banded together and studied regularly with each other for our coursework and our qualifying exams. We also took courses together. We found out that the professor who writes the qualifying exam is the one who just taught the course on that subject. For example, if the qualifying exam covers measure theory, then the professor who taught the previous semester's graduate course on measure theory writes the exam.

Once we figured out this pattern, we decided to make sure we took the class from the professor who would write the qualifying exam for that topic. Our group went to class and studied every day all summer, and I definitely was a regular participant in this group because I did not want to make the same mistakes I had before and barely pass. The math department held two qualifiers at the end of the summer, which covered measure theory and abstract algebra. However, despite my best efforts, and those of our study group, I and one other person unfortunately failed both of these exams.

In the wake of this disappointing outcome, the other person decided that the graduate math program was too much for him and he joined the negative statistic list: he left graduate school at the end of the year without finishing his degree. I was indeed upset about my failure; however, I did not let that deter me from accomplishing my goal of obtaining a PhD. I did not let my initial failure stop me from realizing my objective. Even though others passed their exams the first time, I did not compare myself to them and allow myself to think that they were just naturally smarter and more capable than I. No matter what, I was determined to be a positive statistic, a number within the graduate students of my institution who finished their PhD. So I found another study group and I focused on shoring up my knowledge of these weak areas. If I had decided to think like my fellow classmate, I also might have chosen to get out of graduate school. If I had given in to a defeatist mentality instead of reassuring myself and building my confidence in my ability as a mathematician, I could have given up on my dream. But I was very aware that negative thinking and self-doubt cause failure; positive thinking and determined focus bring success.

So I knuckled down again and hit the books. When the next exam session came around, I felt ready. I had studied very hard and I knew the material inside and out. Although I used the entire time allotted for each exam, the second time around I passed them both with a good grade. A huge weight went off me when I got the good news. I realized then and there that if I could accomplish this task, then I could repeat this focused behavior and succeed at getting the PhD. I also realized that most anyone can achieve an advanced degree as long as he or she is willing to work hard and see it through to its positive end.

As Sean relates, he did not let the initial failure of his exams keep him down. His philosophy was "If at first you don't succeed, try try again," which, regardless of its timeworn nature, in the end did work for him as it has for countless others. It takes emotional maturity to repeat an exam, and even more when one must repeat the exam several times.

As shown in the previous narratives, with fortitude, success can be achieved. In the next story, Jamelle discusses her experience with her cumulative exams. She also found a study group to work with, just as Sean had done, and also found that several tries were needed to get her to her goal. Here is her story.

Do It Again

Jamelle: As an undergraduate, I attended a historically black college and university, where I was used to being the cream of the academic crop. When I got to Purdue and was ready to cut my supposedly sharp intellectual teeth on my graduate level cumulative exams, I realized I still had some things to learn about test-taking and I was not as prepared for graduate school as I had thought. Passing one's cumulative exams or "cumes," as they are fondly called by graduate students in chemistry, is no small accomplishment. I went through several painful failures before I finally joined the cumulative exam hall of fame.

In my graduate chemistry program, the cumes are omnipresent from the beginning of the program. Each student has to pass a cumulative exam in each of the five major areas of chemistry. The exams are given once a month and students have two years to pass in all five areas. I was not sure how to prepare for the first cumulative exam I was going to take, but being full of my undergrad bravado, I diligently holed up in my apartment and studied old lab notes and cumulative exams from senior graduate students and fully devoted myself to mastering the material. Much to my disappointment, I didn't pass my first exam. Since I knew I had studied hard and done my best, I considered the possibility that I might not be studying properly. Obviously, I was doing something wrong.

I decided to reach out to my grad student colleagues who were sitting in the same boat as me—they still needed to pass their cumes. We all agreed that forming a study group was a good idea, so we met weekly to prepare. Much to our disappointment, none of us passed our exams. This process repeated itself, and after many, many (too many to count) monthly tries, finally in the last session, which was in April, I passed one of the exams. By this time, however, my bravado had turned to discouragement, and I didn't know exactly what to do. All of my peers who were not in my study group had passed all of their exams and put their cumes behind them.

Out of the force of sheer determination, those of us in our study group who had yet to pass our cumes buckled down that summer and dedicated ourselves to passing these exams, no matter what. After we spent the whole summer studying, we walked into the first exam in September prepared and excited to pass our cumulatives. All that work almost paid off. Everyone passed but me, and I was devastated. I threw myself a pity party for a while, wallowing in my failure. I am not comfortable in the victim mode, however, so I soon bounced back and rededicated myself to my studies and to succeeding with my exams.

Repetition often is the cure, and combined with yet another round of full-forced dedication to my preparation, in January I consecutively and very proudly passed all four of my exams. I threw a huge victory party, reveling in my success. I had not given up, and I did succeed. I now have graduated with a PhD in chemistry and am successfully employed as a researcher for a major biomedical company.

CONCLUSION

Completing the first year of graduate school is a significant accomplishment and, as these stories have shown, it requires the courage to ask for support, willpower and determination and, simply put, true grit. In this chapter,

Christy, Lauren, Jamelle, and Sean have shared their experiences as first-year doctoral students and the strategies they used not only to survive but to thrive in the face of adversity. They established their identities in their respective departments by maintaining their integrity and self-confidence. Amid some real disappointments and occasional failures, they were able to persevere and successfully complete the first year of graduate school, and consequently to succeed in their PhD programs. Juggling different combinations of research, coursework, and teaching made the mastery of social balance and time management important aspects of their first-year experiences. Though each hurdle appeared insurmountable when encountered, overcoming them allowed these students to experience success and proved to be well worth the effort. Completing the first year of their doctoral programs changed their lives and set Christy, Lauren, Jamelle, and Sean on the path toward successfully completing their PhD degrees.

CHAPTER 2 GROUP DISCUSSION

The first year of graduate school presents significant challenges to students new to graduate school life. New priorities, new relationships, and a demanding work schedule can be overwhelming. As the authors of chapter 2 have made clear, one of the most important skills in navigating the first year of graduate school is the ability to meet adversity such that you clearly establish your brand, or identity, within your academic department. Having a solid sense of who you are in your department academically and socially, and talking through the issues presented in this chapter as part of a group discussion, can help increase your ability to complete the manifold requirements necessary for success in your graduate program.

A number of materials have been created to stimulate thoughtful discussion about the chapter topic, including a video titled *Overheard in the Office*. The video scenario takes place in a graduate student office that is shared by a first-year graduate student, Brendan, and several senior graduate students. Brendan finds himself in a precarious position, which is the stimulus for creative thought and group conversation. The video and accompanying materials for leading a group discussion on this chapter can be downloaded from the chapter 2 resource web page at http://dx.doi.org/10.5703/1288284315198.

CHAPTER AUTHOR PROFILES

Christy L. Erving

Ms. Erving was born and raised in Dallas, Texas, and aspired from a very young age to be an attorney, which prompted her to attend a law magnet high school in Dallas. As a first-generation college student, Ms. Erving lost her passion for studying law when she participated in an undergraduate study abroad program in the Dominican Republic and saw firsthand the health needs of its socially disadvantaged population. She became very interested in issues of race, immigration, and health inequalities and subsequently graduated from Rice University with a bachelor's degree in sociology and Hispanic studies. She then enrolled in the doctoral program in Indiana University's Department of Sociology, where she is focusing on medical sociology. Currently a PhD candidate, Ms. Erving is teaching and writing her dissertation, which examines the co-occurrence of physical and mental health problems across various racial and ethnic groups in the United States.

Lauren J. Parker

Ms. Parker was born in High Point, North Carolina, and later moved to Manassas, Virginia. The oldest of three, she is a natural born leader and has always had a passion to help others. A product of the Prince William County educational system, Ms. Parker attended Hampton University to complete her undergraduate studies. While at Hampton she majored in sociology and participated in the Ronald E. McNair Program at the University of Tennessee Knoxville, as well as both the Summer Research Opportunity Program and Alliance for Graduate Education and Professoriate (AGEP) Summer Bridge Program at Purdue University. Although her first love will always be sociology, Ms. Parker earned a master's degree in public health with a concentration in community health at Purdue University and is now completing a PhD in health and kinesiology/gerontology at Purdue.

Jamelle K. P. Williams, PhD

Dr. Williams was born and raised in Mobile, Alabama. She attended public schools for most of her life until she began her collegiate career at the prestigious Tuskegee University. After completing her degree at Tuskegee, she enrolled at Purdue University to obtain her PhD in chemistry. Her time at Purdue can best be described as painstaking, yet rewarding. She successfully finished her PhD in chemistry and is currently working for a research company in Alabama. Her ultimate goal in life is to give back to her community.

Sean A. Colbert-Kelly, PhD

Dr. Colbert-Kelly received his PhD in mathematics from Purdue University. His dissertation work involved conducting research in the area of calculus of variations as applicable to Ginzburg-Landau-type functionals. Originally from Maryland, he attended a national blue ribbon high school where he participated in the science and technology program. He later attended the University of Maryland, Baltimore County (UMBC), and was a participant in the Meyerhoff Scholarship Program. Dr. Colbert-Kelly has always excelled academically and striven to participate in competitive programs that would take him to the next level. While at UMBC he discovered his love for mathematics. He is currently working as a mathematics researcher at the National Institute of Standards and Technology, conducting research in fluid dynamics and interfacial rheology.

Chapter 3

Choosing a Thesis Advisor: Surprise and Success

Kermin Joel Hernández, PhD

←——————————————————————→

INTRODUCTION

One of the most daunting and yet important decisions in graduate school is the selection of your thesis advisor. Inviting an advisor into your graduate thesis process is like hiring a ship navigator who will help guide your graduate study through the sometimes choppy waters of data research and thesis writing and into the safe harbor of graduation and a good job. Although you remain the captain of your own career, your graduate advisor teaches you how to use the charts and equipment that will bring you to the completion of your graduate degree.

The specific steps involved in choosing an advisor vary according to department and school; however, some aspects of this process are universal, no matter which college or university you attend. Many people compare this selection process to choosing a spouse, because the thesis advisor is someone who will be with you, directly or indirectly, throughout your professional life.

As in finding and forging any successful professional relationship, identifying a compatible advisor is not an easy task, and few road maps exist that explain how to manage it. Consequently, most graduate students begin the process of choosing their thesis advisor without much background information. A lack of preparation can lead to disappointing results, whereas an informed approach can achieve a very satisfying outcome. In fact, a compatible advisor can function as your career navigator, someone you can consult for professional advice whenever your career takes an unexpected turn or presents a promising opportunity. In the end, the rewards that come with a reliable advisor who is right for you, your professional goals, and your field of study, are worth the investment of extra time and energy in a thorough search process.

In the stories that follow, I offer you some insight into this sometimes unpredictable quest and share my decision-making process, as well as a few of the experiences I have had in my search for thesis advisors. I hope this chapter will prepare you to choose an advisor who will work well with you and see you through to the completion of your graduate degree.

STARTING YOUR ADVISOR SEARCH

The logical first step in choosing a graduate thesis advisor is identifying a professor in your area of interest with whom you believe you would work well. This requires having a clear focus in terms of your field of interest. When you have determined the area you wish to study, the process of identifying your preferred thesis advisor can often start with a combination of things: advice from your undergraduate professors, your own research and planning, and as my narrative will show, a certain amount of luck and being ready to respond to an opportunity when it presents itself.

I believe that finding the right advisor is an organic process that develops out of interests and the connections you have made in your undergraduate program. This process often begins in your undergraduate years when you start to search for the college or university that you want to attend and the graduate program that matches your research interests. In my case, I was certain of where I wanted to study, and that certainty led me to find my graduate thesis advisor unexpectedly. My story is an example of getting to know one's advisor before entering graduate school, as I did before I began my master's program. Finding an advisor who aligned with my personality and research interests was the key to my successful advisor/graduate student relationship. My story starts with my bachelor's degree program, because the chain of events and connections that led to my area of interest, and then my graduate advisor, started there. In it I share how I met my advisors, how I made my decision to work with them, and how these advisors became my valuable colleagues.

Good Things Are Sometimes Found in Unexpected Places

My story begins during the second year of my bachelor's degree program. I was taking an analytical chemistry course to complete my program requirements when a new instructor, Dr. García-Díaz, was assigned to teach the class. He seemed to be an amicable guy, and he had a lot of passion for chemistry and his research. I remember that around sixty-five students were in that classroom without air conditioning in August, and oh boy—it was hot! We were sweating like crazy, but we still paid close attention to the new professor because he was interesting and seemed to have much to offer us as students.

At that time I had no clue as to what specifically I wanted to do as a chemist, and then to my surprise, I fell in love with analytical chemistry in that class. The way this professor explained the concepts and the applications was fantastic and enough to motivate me fully and spark my desire to look deeper into analytical chemistry as a field of study. Maybe his passion for the field was the fuel that sparked my interest in it, or maybe it was his honesty about his life experiences and his unique way of bringing relevant topics from the real world into the classroom. Not every professor does a good job of connecting everyday life with the scientific topics discussed in class, but in this regard Dr. García-Díaz gave it his best shot every time and was always right on target.

Because his enthusiasm rubbed off on me, I did very well in that class and recognized that Dr. García-Díaz was someone with whom I wanted to work more. I looked up his research interests on the department website, and I became even more convinced that I wanted to work with him when I found that he studied natural compounds in medicinal plants, a topic I was very interested in studying. So, in meeting Dr. García-Díaz I had not only found someone I wanted to work with, but also discovered my major area of academic interest.

The next step in finding my advisor, according to university policy, was for me to request a position in Dr. García-Díaz's lab. I approached him to see if he would accept me and we ended up chatting for about two hours in his office. He talked about his research, his family, and life in general. I learned then that he was very personable and a pro-student professor. Most importantly, he said he would be happy to have me work in his lab for my junior and senior research courses. We then discussed several possible research topics that we could explore, and one of them really struck my interest: analyzing endemic plants from Puerto Rico to verify their medicinal properties. I had grown up with a mother who grew herbs and medicinal plants in our backyard, and I was always fascinated with the way various illnesses responded to these plant remedies. We ended our conversation on a very positive note. He involved me right away in his current project, asking me to research the background of verbena (*Stachytarpheta jamaicensis*), a plant he was interested in investigating. We agreed to meet the following week to go over my findings.

I spent that week at the library reading background information on verbena and its properties. Unfortunately the library did not have very much to offer, but I did find materials online at other libraries. So, I went to the information desk and asked a librarian for help. She told me I needed to order these materials from interlibrary loan, which could take several weeks. (Back in those days, interlibrary loan worked as it does now, but it was much slower.) Although it would be frustrating to wait that long, I realized that the wait would be okay, even if I didn't like it much. I had to meet with my professor the next day and I would have to show up empty-handed.

Walking back to the chemistry building, I was thinking about this nerve-wracking situation when I saw my friend Miguel, who asked me how things were going. I told him that Dr. García-Díaz wanted me to research something and I just found out it was going to take forever to get what I need from interlibrary loan. He said, "You will get it, don't worry. They are slow, but eventually you will get it. I did it one time and it took just a month." I guess I had to be patient, but I didn't look forward to telling Dr. García-Díaz that I hadn't been successful in finding much on verbena. So, I went home and tried to relax a little and prepare for my meeting the next day.

Much to my surprise, Dr. García-Díaz was pleased with my progress even though, as far as I was concerned, I was unable to do much. He said, "Don't worry, this is part of being a scientist. You need to be patient. You did a good job finding what you needed and ordering it." So, that made me feel very good and I was reassured of my decision to work with him. Then, also unexpectedly, he offered me a job in his lab during the summer. Needless to say, I immediately took him up on it.

Another Great Surprise

As it turned out, I was able to get funding for my work with Dr. García-Díaz in the summer through the Louis Stokes Alliances for Minority Participation (LSAMP). I found out about this funding opportunity when I noticed a bright orange flyer on the department bulletin board by the main office. It was covered with a crowded patchwork of flyers advertising all kinds of different learning opportunities and study programs. I remember that the orange flyer said: "Research Summer Experience, stipend available." Later, when I was talking with our department's academic advisor, she mentioned the LSAMP program, so I went back and looked at the information on the flyer again, and there was the LSAMP website. I looked it up right away. The description of the program spoke to my career interests, and I met the qualifications for it. I went ahead and applied, hoping for the best. I was elated when I actually received the fellowship and told Dr. García-Díaz about it in my next meeting with him.

He was very excited that I was able to find funding for my work and told me that I could start working right away on his latest research idea, this time involving the characterization of the chemical compounds found in the verbena plant. I accepted this challenge. In the meantime, while waiting for my interlibrary loans to arrive, I was patient but not idle. I purchased some reagents and other materials that I needed and began the work as far as I could. Three weeks later, the interlibrary loan materials finally arrived, and I was able to learn more about the plant properties and other research that had been done on them.

I continued with this research for the following two years of my undergraduate program and learned the basics of scientific research procedures and instrumentation techniques in analytical chemistry. It was exciting to get involved with a lab so early in my career and learn the ups and downs of chemistry research. The downs dominated parts of the journey, but Dr. García-Díaz helped me understand that disappointments were part of the process. He often remarked: "99 percent of experiments don't work out, but the successful 1 percent have made great contributions to science."

After working with me for several months, Dr. García-Díaz saw my potential as a researcher and encouraged me to continue with the master's program in chemistry after I finished my BS degree. I applied to the chemistry program there at the University of Puerto Rico–Mayagüez (UPR–Mayagüez) and was accepted. Naturally, I selected Dr. García-Díaz as my advisor for my master's thesis, even while I was still finishing my undergraduate research projects. I was grateful to find my master's thesis advisor in this way. Since I had taken a class with him and gotten to know him while I was an undergraduate, I knew I had a good rapport with him before I asked him to be my advisor for my master's project.

Throughout my master's program, Dr. García-Díaz facilitated my development as a researcher and coached me in gaining the skills I needed to be successful in scientific research. I liked his honesty about research and his patience in dealing with me as a student attempting to learn. He was a good listener and open to advising me on things besides my research, like personal issues and life difficulties. I discovered he was wise in many ways. He also trained me to advise younger graduate and undergraduate students regarding their research. I became pretty much in charge of running his lab and making sure that it was properly stocked with all the materials and supplies needed to operate efficiently. Dr. García-Díaz always encouraged my attending national conferences to present research, both at the undergraduate and graduate levels. He also challenged me regularly. He knew, for instance, that I was not good in English, but he encouraged me to move beyond my comfort zone and to not be shy. I met his challenges and worked hard at putting together conference presentations in English, even though I felt awkward doing so. I am grateful to him for having pushed me like this, because it really helped my public speaking and my spoken English skills.

Very grateful for Dr. García-Díaz's mentorship, I successfully graduated with my MS in chemistry. Thanks to the years that I worked in his lab and the rapport that he and I developed, we still have a good relationship today, even though he wanted me to continue as an analytical chemist, and I chose instead to study chemical education. Every time I go back to visit my family and friends in Puerto Rico, I meet with him and we talk for hours. He has become more than an advisor to me. I consider him a friend, a colleague, a mentor, and a role model. Not only did Dr. García-Díaz's mentoring greatly facilitate my success in the MS program at UPR–Mayagüez, his encouragement to attend conferences also led me to my PhD thesis advisor.

The Right Place at the Right Time

Some people might find their PhD advisor very logically, through a referral or through a focused search of the literature in their area of interest. Others might find their advisor randomly when they are not even looking and in places that they hadn't anticipated, such as a professional conference, which was where I met mine.

When I was in the master's program at UPR-Mayagüez, I attended a major chemistry conference to present a paper in the beautiful city of Ponce, Puerto Rico, where I loved to breathe in the fresh shoreline breezes of the Caribbean Sea. At that time I was also applying to graduate school for my doctoral degree. I was interested in doing my PhD studies in chemical education, and Purdue University was my first choice because I had been advised by one of my professors that Purdue was a pioneer in the chemical education field. I didn't have any idea where Purdue was, so I also didn't know it is located in a small city quite far away from everything except soybean and corn fields. I knew it had a prestigious reputation, so I was very interested in studying there.

As I sat on the conference center veranda in Ponce looking out over the shining blue waters of the bay, I finally had the time to read through the conference program in detail, and to my surprise, one of the speakers was Dr. Kathryn Henderson, a professor of chemical education from Purdue University. What a great coincidence! For me, her presence there in Puerto Rico was pure chance, random and unexpected. You can call this moment serendipity or just simply luck, but it happened at the right time and the right place, and much to my advantage. Even though attending conferences took time and energy amid the work of graduate school, I knew then why Dr. García-Díaz always got me to attend these events.

I wrote down the time and location of Dr. Henderson's presentation and made sure I attended. Her talk was great. She discussed her research—the use of technology as an educational tool. I liked her work very much and was eager to learn more about it. I spoke with her after her paper presentation and told her about my sincere interest in attending Purdue's program in chemical education. Speaking English with Dr. Henderson was a challenge, but I did my best with my exotic accent (as some have referred to it) to make sure she realized that I was very interested in her work. We spoke briefly, because others were waiting to speak with her, but she gave me her business card so that I could follow up by e-mail. I had just met a person who was going to play a major role in my life, and I had nothing to do with finding her, except that I had worked very intensively to get my paper ready for that conference. Now it looked like my hard work was paying off in unexpected ways.

Welcome to the Sea of Green

Directly after the conference, with help from friends with my English, I followed through and e-mailed Dr. Henderson with my questions about the chemical education program at Purdue. Her positive response confirmed for me that I wanted to do my PhD studies at Purdue University. The rest just sort of went according to plan as I followed Purdue's graduate school application procedures. I applied and was accepted, and I made arrangements for a campus visit. One thing I did that was very important: I contacted Dr. Henderson by e-mail in advance of my trip so that I could set up a meeting and speak with her in person while I was there. Let me tell you that I revised that e-mail many times and asked my friends to proofread it to make sure it was correct. I didn't want to give the wrong impression; I knew that my English needed work. In this e-mail I reminded Dr. Henderson about the conversation we had in Puerto Rico and the e-mails we had already exchanged so that she would remember me. (Whenever I follow up with contacts I make at conferences, I am careful to mention where we met.) This advance planning worked out. I heard back from her well before I left for Purdue and we set up a meeting that accommodated both of our schedules.

Everything seemed to be coming together magically until I was driving to the airport to get my plane at San Juan to fly to Indianapolis, Indiana—the closest airport to West Lafayette. I was so excited about my campus visit that I didn't realize I was speeding. The next thing I knew, I was pulled over. The police officer was not kind. No warning—he gave me a $120 speeding ticket. What bad luck. I slowed down and tried to keep thinking positively that everything would be all right, but reflecting on it later I realized that this speeding ticket was foreshadowing some of the surprises waiting for me at Purdue. At that point, however, I just kept telling myself, "I just have to get to Purdue and everything will be okay." Fortunately, my visit from the traffic cop didn't make me late, and I still made my flight, which was about six hours long. I finally arrived in Indianapolis and learned that I had to take a limo to West Lafayette. When the ground transport lady told me about it, I was thinking, "Wow—a limo, really? That sounds nice."

Well as often is the case, it took longer than expected to get my bags, and the next thing I knew I was running like mad to make it on time to the place where the limo stopped for passengers. I made it okay, but then, guess what.

I found myself standing inside this boxy, old-fashioned shuttle bus with another twenty people or so, more or less jammed into this odd version of a limo! And, I didn't realize that I would be inside this little box on wheels for at least an hour.

The ride from the airport to West Lafayette was kind of wild with a nutty, annoying driver, who accelerated and decelerated constantly throughout the whole trip. I hoped that all of this was not a premonition of my graduate school experience to come. As it turned out, some of this start and stop craziness would actually continue.

After we left the Indianapolis city limits I noticed a new color surrounding me: rich and vibrant green. Many little farms with their wide fields of beans and corn stretched as far as the eye could see. I felt like I was a pioneer heading west, even though we were headed north. Finally, after twenty-something stops in the little towns along the way, around nine o'clock at night, a bigger town appeared. We had arrived in West Lafayette at the Purdue Memorial Union Hotel. None of the insanity I endured on my trip mattered now. I found my room, crashed onto my bed, and slept so I would be ready and alert for my campus visit the next day.

I woke up early in the morning and, using a campus map, located the chemistry department and headed across campus for meetings with various professors and administrators. Later that day, I went to the appointment that I had set up with Dr. Henderson. I made it a point to find her office and be there waiting to meet her well ahead of time. She was glad to see me and said in the interview that she wanted to accept me into her research group, but then explained that I needed to follow the department protocol when I arrived in the fall before being assigned to a particular lab. She said that this protocol involved sitting in on at least eight faculty members' introductory lectures explaining their research. She highly encouraged me to put her name as my first choice on the forms I had to fill out. After meeting with her, I felt pretty confident that I would be able to get her as my advisor, but I wasn't so sure about the eight introductory lectures I had to sit in on. I decided that, as always, I would worry about it when the time came and then do my best to succeed. On the whole, the campus visit went very well, and I felt I was almost sure of a place in Dr. Henderson's lab, if I followed all of the details of the department protocol as she had explained.

The next day, I boarded the lovely limo back to the Indianapolis airport and arrived in plenty of time for my return trip to San Juan, which went via

Miami. Unfortunately, the airplane had mechanical problems, and my flight was delayed for an hour or so. By the time we got going, I had barely enough time to make my Miami connection, which was with a different airline. As soon as I got to Miami, I took off running to the other terminal but missed my connection. Darn it! Then, just to add a little more spice to the story, the airline didn't have any seats on any other flight that night to San Juan. And, no matter how much I pleaded, they didn't want to pay for my overnight stay. According to them, I had flown with a different airline from Indianapolis, and so my situation "was not their fault." This meant I had to pay for my hotel—not fun! I begged the agent to put me on the earliest flight to San Juan. Fortunately she felt compassion for me and found me a seat on the very next flight at 5:30 the following morning. Great, I was all set with my flight. Now all I needed was to find a hotel. I went outside and waved down a taxi and asked him to drop me at a hotel that he could recommend. I also made a reservation with him to pick me up the next morning at 3:30 a.m., so that I wouldn't miss my flight.

Off we went to his version of a hotel. I don't know what that taxi driver was thinking. He dropped me off at a motel that I don't want to remember. True, they had rooms available for a *very* affordable price, too good to be true, in fact. I was too tired to deal with looking for another place, so I checked in and found the so-called room. When I tried to close the door, it wouldn't shut completely, let alone lock. The room smelled like smoke, and the air conditioner made this weird squeaky noise. The bathroom, especially the bathtub, was kind of dirty and certainly not a place for a pleasant shower. I ended up going to the nearby drugstore to buy some cleanser to clean the tub, and I still wore my flip-flops in the shower. What a nightmare! I didn't sleep that well, thinking that someone would open the door of my room at any moment. I woke up at 3:00 a.m. the next morning and was outside at 3:30 waiting for the taxi driver, but even after several phone calls, he never showed up.

I nervously called another taxi, which came quickly (thank heaven), and I managed to get to the airport on time but not early enough to eat breakfast or even buy a granola bar. With no meal served on the flight, I starved. At least I was able to rest a little on the plane. Once we landed in San Juan I headed straight for the donuts and coffee in the terminal. Then I grabbed my luggage and found my car, which I had safely parked in the airport lot, and with a few extra donuts and my coffee refill, I started my two and a half hour drive back to Mayagüez, car windows down and gratefully inhaling the clean breeze from my beautiful island's seashores. After an hour or so, I was happily singing along with a very famous salsa song on the radio, "Así Es La Mujer Que Amo" ("This Is the Woman That I Love"), when I slowed down to stop at a traffic light and noticed in my mirror the blue flashing lights of a police car, again! I was thinking maybe something had happened somewhere else and he would pass me, but no, I was wrong. He sounded his siren and pulled me over.

I started to laugh out loud and the police officer asked me what I was laughing about. "What is so funny?" he questioned. I said, "Señor, this is unbelievable. It has nothing to do with you. I am just laughing to avoid crying." I continued, "I am going to put a concrete block under my gas pedal because I was just pulled over three days ago on my way to the airport to go to a campus visit at Purdue University. And tonight, I am returning back home and here I get pulled over again." He just said, "Well, you were speeding!" and proceeded to give me a $130 ticket. Apparently, the dutiful police officer didn't appreciate my Purdue story. What ridiculously bad luck. I just hoped that this trend was only temporary. I consoled myself thinking about my campus visit to Purdue and all of its memorable moments. Trying not to think about the eight miscellaneous lectures I would have to attend, I felt confident I could rest assured that I had successfully set myself up with an excellent advisor for my PhD studies. Unfortunately, I was stuck in debt for a while with the grungy hotel bill and the hefty $250 in speeding fines, but these costs were just a minor setback. I was accepted by Purdue University's chemistry department and that was all that mattered to me.

After my Purdue campus visit and my airport odyssey, it was time to refocus on my studies. For the remainder of the semester and the rest of the summer, I finished my master's thesis, graduated with my master's degree, and got organized for my PhD program at Purdue. Also at that time, and while I was writing my master's thesis, I was preparing for my wedding with my wonderful fiancée, Nahyr, whom I had met during a chemical education conference in San Juan a year earlier. I had been singing about a real person when I was speeding down that road. We decided to get married on July 21, just before we would move to West Lafayette and Purdue. We returned from our honeymoon on July 27, and by August 1 we were unpacking our things in West Lafayette, Indiana. Fortunately travel woes had not continued to plague us. The fall semester would soon begin, and I was very excited to be starting graduate school in a PhD program.

A Few Clouds, a Silver Lining

During the first week in my new PhD program, I set up a meeting with Dr. Henderson and spoke with her in person. I mentioned again my interest in being part of her research group, and she reminded me again of the protocol I needed to follow in order to get into her lab. She said that the details were all explained in the department handbook. I thanked her for her instruction, but in fact I was seriously frustrated. I wanted to bypass these eight lectures. I was being subtly asked to slow down—a message that I had unfortunately heard before from two traffic cops outside of San Juan. I just wanted to move forward and grab my opportunity to work with Dr. Henderson. I knew I wanted her as my advisor. What if something went wrong with the process, and she didn't get assigned to me? I wanted a commitment! But no matter how nice I was, how great my application for the program was, or how organized and responsible I may have seemed, all she did was tell me about the department handbook I had to read. She was as strict as the traffic cop with his little pad of tickets.

At the graduate student orientation, I finally received the handbook, which indeed explained the details about the chemistry department's procedure for selecting a thesis advisor. This process requires all of the chemistry department professors to give presentations throughout the fall semester that introduce their research interests to the new graduate students. Each student must attend eight of these talks. Then the student selects the top three that interest him or her the most, fills out the necessary paperwork, and hopes for the best. Well, no way around it, I had to slow down. The eight lectures had to be my next step.

Let me tell you, sitting through these talks was very time consuming, tedious, and in some instances downright boring. The whole process took about two months. Since only four of the research talks I attended were related to chemistry education, this meant that I needed to attend four others that did not interest me at all. However, I was patient during this process and hung in there, hoping that I would get my first choice of advisor and the lab I knew I wanted. Despite these delays, I did not lose sight of my final destination.

If listening to research talks not related to my field of interest was boring, the competition to get into the lab of my choice made up for this lack of excitement. Because at that time the department had only four professors in chemical education, and only three were accepting new graduate students, there were many more students than there were places in the labs. Let me clarify that even though the graduate student indicates that a certain professor is his or her first choice, this selection does not guarantee that the professor will accept the student into his or her research group. It's sort of like getting onto the airport limo, but without a guarantee that the limo will stop at the destination named on your ticket. Consequently, a certain amount of politics gets involved in this selection process, and some graduate students do not play fair in this game. Though their behavior is not admirable, it is understandable because everyone wants to get his or her first choice of the available labs. Some graduate students can do extreme things in order to be accepted in research groups, and frequently a good deal of drama transpires during the placement process of graduate students with suitable labs and advisors. Some of my colleagues had not made contact with an advisor in advance the way I did, and these people ended up joining research groups other than their first choice.

Since I knew beforehand which professor I wanted to work with, and since I had introduced myself to Dr. Henderson in advance so that she knew me and wanted me in her lab, in the end things worked out the way I wanted them to. Thank goodness she accepted me into her research group. Most importantly, I am happy to share with you that I successfully completed my program and obtained my PhD in chemical education with Dr. Henderson, whose instruction and guidance was second to none.

The energy you put into learning about graduate programs and their faculty, the clear and timely communication you have with the professors you are interested in working with, and your patience in going through the sometimes tedious process of selecting an advisor will all pay off in the end. I can assure you that the skills I learned from my doctoral work became assets for my postdoctoral position. Being able to show that I could work with an interdisciplinary group of researchers helped me tremendously during my interview and work as a postdoctoral researcher.

I highly advise those who are considering a graduate degree in the sciences to do your homework in advance of choosing a graduate advisor. Read articles written by the professor that you want to work with, meet in advance with the professor in person if at all possible, and verify whether or not you "click." Visit the professor's research group and talk with other graduate and postdoctoral students. Ask if it would be permissible to follow along with their research group for a day or two, and while there, ask as many questions as possible. Remember, the professor in charge of this lab will be the person advising you for the next four or more years of your life, so you need to be very wise about selecting the best possible fit for yourself as you choose a thesis advisor and research program.

In looking back, I think my early knowledge that I wanted to go to Purdue, reaching out to meet my future thesis advisor at that conference, and then going out of my way to meet her again during my campus visit, contributed to my being accepted into her lab. I was also fortunate enough to choose advisors, both in my master's and PhD programs, who helped me develop a set of skills beyond my major area of research. Having these skills allowed me to demonstrate to my future colleagues that I could work outside of my comfort zone. For example, I started as an analytical chemist for my master's, then I switched gears to chemical education with an emphasis in video gaming. So, I was well equipped to do research and assessment in a nontraditional environment. Although I didn't realize their full value at the time, the skills I gained working with my two advisors in two different fields paved the way for my postdoctoral position in educational outreach in nanotechnology. I was able to use all the skills I developed during graduate school in my postdoctoral position. And, having these skills increased the likelihood I would land a tenure track job. Consequently, I am happy to tell you that I have recently accepted a tenure track teaching position and I will soon begin my first semester as an assistant professor in chemistry at a teaching-oriented liberal arts school in upstate New York.

CONCLUSION

The story related in this chapter provides some key insights into choosing the right thesis advisor who can make your graduate program an exciting and rewarding academic experience. Finding this advisor requires that you know quite clearly the topic and direction you want to pursue in graduate school, so that the choice of the advisor can be as informed as possible. This process might be different from one department or institution to the next, but I believe my story is relevant to most graduate students who are about to embark on the search for the program and advisor that will be best for them. The takeaway message from this chapter is to think proactively when preparing to attend graduate school. Plan the selection of your advisor as much as possible. Do not wait until you get into graduate school to start this process; do your homework beforehand. This proactive thinking and planning will ensure that you have a rewarding graduate school experience. Your advance efforts will definitely pay off in the end.

CHAPTER 3 GROUP DISCUSSION

Finding an excellent graduate thesis advisor requires a focused career objective and advance planning. In his chapter, Kermin provides many examples of his proactive approach to choosing a thesis advisor. Although an informed search for an advisor is often the best strategy, even the best-laid plans can be unexpectedly disrupted through no fault of the student.

In the video for this chapter, titled *Changes*, you will listen in as members of an entire lab group learn that their thesis advisor has accepted a faculty position at another university and will be moving the lab. Dealing with unexpected changes is also a part of graduate student life. The discussion activity created for this chapter will give you a chance to practice dealing with unexpected changes and the process of sorting out your available options in their wake. The video and accompanying materials for leading a group discussion on this chapter can be downloaded from the chapter 3 resource web page at http://dx.doi.org/10.5703/1288284315200.

CHAPTER AUTHOR PROFILE

Kermin Joel Hernández, PhD

Dr. Hernández earned his BS and MS degrees in chemistry at the University of Puerto Rico–Mayagüez and graduated with a PhD degree in chemical education from Purdue University. After graduation he took a postdoctoral position in nanotechnology education at the Interdisciplinary Education Group of the University of Wisconsin–Madison's Materials Research Science and Engineering Center. While there he developed nanotechnology educational materials as well as general science education curricula, outreach programs, and classroom activities. In addition, he has been a committed leader for several years within the Society for the Advancement of Chicanos and Native Americans in Science (SACNAS). Dr. Hernández is currently an assistant professor of chemistry at St. John Fisher College, where he teaches general chemistry classes and organizes differentiated instruction and problem-based learning workshops for teachers.

Chapter 4

Choosing a Thesis Advisor: Familiar Paths and Unexpected Curves

Nahyr D. Rovira-Figueroa, PhD

INTRODUCTION

Graduate school is often like a great forest with many unfamiliar pathways; sometimes you can see the way clearly ahead, and other times the forest is bigger than the individual trees along the way. For this reason, as the previous chapter also advised, you need to know as much as possible about your graduate program and the advisor you are considering before you set off on your PhD journey. You need a trustworthy and competent guide to turn to when you are not sure whether the path is going to lead to the other side of the woods, or just in a circle. My inspiration and dedication to my work and the powerful ideals I had developed at an early age, in conjunction with my choices of graduate advisors, proved to be essential in preserving my long-term goals as a researcher and educator in chemistry. As my story will attest, the path to a graduate degree and its completion requires that you maintain a steadfast vision of your goal and fortitude in the face of obstacles.

PERSISTENCE AND A GOOD ADVISOR ARE THE MOTHERS OF SUCCESS

The stories I have to share about my graduate advisor experiences tell about both the moments when my path through graduate school was unobstructed, and the moments when my path was obscured. I share my story about my early beginnings as a young research scientist, and then continue to my undergraduate degree program and tell how I found a wonderful advisor who mentored me through my first MS program at the University of Puerto Rico–Mayagüez (UPR–Mayagüez). I relate how my love of chemistry, fostered at an early age, sustained me when I faced challenges in finding the right graduate advisor in my PhD program at Purdue University. My recollections will show you how my steadfast commitment to my goals, despite the obstacles I had to surmount, helped me to develop a solid graduate career and obtain a PhD in chemical education. Here is my story.

Inspiring Are the Seeds That Grow Indoors

When I was in high school in Ponce, biology and chemistry fascinated me. And because I was so enthusiastic about these subjects, I was given the opportunity to conduct a science project involving the design of a hydroponic system to grow plants indoors. Working on this project inspired me to enroll in a chemistry class at school. With the help of Dr. González, a chemical engineer, and my father, also a chemist, I worked for an entire year building a hydroponic garden system. It could hold forty-eight bean plants and could also adjust the concentration and type of nutrients that each plant received. I entered my project in the school science fair and won first prize—an achievement of which I am still very proud. My project was then nominated for the district, regional, and state science fair competitions. At the district science fair competition I won first place, and at the regional competition I won second.

Although I didn't win an award at the state fair, the opportunity to be part of these events was its own reward offering lifelong lessons, including (1) a vivid understanding of the scientific method, (2) a grounding in the conducting of research, (3) the experience of presenting innovative research to a group of well-recognized scientists, and (4) participation in a variety of informal science education experiences. Perhaps the most valuable benefit of this experience was the powerful sense of confidence I gained in myself as a thinker and researcher as a result of these successes. This project was my first introduction to the work chemists and chemical engineers do in real life. I learned that if I applied my intelligence and my dedication to this type of scientific project, I could make a valuable contribution to society. Thus inspired by my engaging interactions with the various scientists I met through my science fair project, I decided that I wanted to do something to foster my newfound desire to study chemistry.

Consequently I pursued my BS degree in chemistry at UPR–Mayagüez. The process of finding my graduate advisor actually began early in my undergraduate career, although like a seed sprouting invisibly under the ground, it was something I wasn't fully aware of. Like many young chemistry majors, I had the idea that I wanted to finish my degree as a chemist and then work in an industrial setting. Then, I received a letter from the UPR–Mayagüez Louis Stokes Alliance for Minority Participation (LSAMP) program coordinator explaining that my academic advisor had nominated me as a possible candidate for the program. His letter stated that my grades and courses showed that I had the potential to be successful in the undergraduate summer research program. I was very happy to get this news and I figured that my success with my hydroponic research project had come along with me to college. But, did I want to join LSAMP? The letter highlighted the positive aspects of conducting undergraduate research. It also stated that it could be an opportunity to do the following: (1) meet fellow students who shared my interests, (2) build my resume, (3) provide a stipend for my work as an undergraduate researcher, and (4) allow me to receive undergraduate research credits. The letter also included an application form and explanation of what the summer research program entailed. I concluded that there was nothing to lose and so applied for it. I filled out the application, asked three of my professors for the required letters of recommendation, and submitted the paperwork. A couple of weeks later I received an acceptance letter from the LSAMP program.

My decision to join LSAMP turned out to be a good one. Being a part of this program and conducting undergraduate research provided me with other professional opportunities. For example, as the letter from LSAMP had anticipated, I did meet other undergraduate students who were conducting research, and with whom I shared similar interests. I became a member of a distinguished group of young scholars who wanted to do research, meet other people in their field, and advance in their careers as scientists. I felt that I was part of something significant, not just another anonymous student on campus.

I also met graduate students and faculty who encouraged me to do research and provided me with feedback on possible career choices other than working in an industrial setting. The world of teaching and research within the scholarly academy opened up to me for the very first time, and I began to realize that I could develop my career in chemistry as a faculty member of a college or university. A new path for my life unfolded before me.

The Seed Sprouts

Then came the practical steps of making this new life direction a reality. As part of the LSAMP program, I was required to select a faculty member with whom I wanted to work for my summer research project and who would then continue as my advisor for the last two years of my BS program. My first reaction to this challenge was one of doubt and confusion, because I barely knew any of the chemistry faculty. The chemistry department was quite large. It had around sixty-five faculty members and ten continuing lecturers. I only knew a few of them because I had only taken two chemistry courses, general and organic chemistry. The general chemistry instructors in the department were continuing lecturers who were not conducting research. And I did not want to work with the organic chemistry professor because he was working on chemical synthesis, and my interests did not lie in this area.

So there I was, facing this huge and complex department. I had to find a faculty member who would be my advisor for the next two years! I didn't even know who these people were, and now I was supposed to interview them. I wasn't certain how I could find them or how to talk to them. So, I decided to determine all my options. I went to the departmental secretary and asked her for a list of the chemistry department's researchers and their research interests, and she advised me to consult the department's newly created website for all of this information. The secretary pointed out that the website listed the faculty members available to serve as advisors for undergraduate students, and those who were interested in mentoring and accepting undergraduates in their research groups.

Her suggestion made answering my questions easy. The website was a very simple one. This was back in 1995, so there were no pictures, just a typed list of the faculty names and specializations. The list contained approximately forty names, highlighted by discipline (such as organic, inorganic, biochemistry, analytical chemistry, and so forth) with brief descriptions of their research interests. I printed out the list and read it carefully, highlighting those research topics that aligned with my interests and my then limited knowledge of chemistry. I narrowed down the list of professors to six possibilities. Since Puerto Rico in 1995 was still in the era before e-mail, the faculty posted their office hours on their door and students simply went and checked these, or they called the professors' secretaries to find out when professors were available for individual student meetings.

At that time, the chemistry department was located in the old chemistry building, so the offices had high ceilings and tall windows. These features brought a sort of character to the whole building's atmosphere, and I enjoyed walking through the old halls and visiting the faculty offices. In the end, I set up my appointments both through the professors' secretaries and in person during their office hours. Being so new to the field I felt insecure and, looking back on it, I think I was more worried about impressing them than finding the perfect mentor. I just wanted to find a good undergraduate research advisor who would accept me as a student researcher and with whom I could work productively and develop a good professional relationship.

Setting up the interviews was for the most part easy to do. Preparing for the appointments both psychologically and practically, however, required some presence of mind, as I will describe. I was thankful that the faculty members honored the appointments that I had set up with them. When I arrived, in most cases, the professor was there waiting for me and would ask me to come in. Some of their offices were very crowded with books and papers, so we walked down the hall and met in a conference room instead. I would show them my acceptance letter to the LSAMP program, tell them that I was looking for a researcher who was willing to accept undergraduate students, and we would then discuss their research interests and project agendas.

In order to sound like I had done my homework and knew what I was talking about, I studied each professor's résumé beforehand and developed questions that I could ask about their research. I also brought along a notebook with questions to ask them, where I could note their responses and the details of our conversations. At the beginning of each interview I was nervous because I didn't know what to expect. I went into the interview with an open attitude, just listening and responding, and doing my best to understand what each of them said to me. As the conversation continued, however, they made me feel comfortable, and I realized that I didn't have to try so hard. After all, they were people who had voluntarily listed themselves as possible advisors and mentors, so they liked talking with and working with undergraduate students.

They were happy to explain their research agendas and give me information about their research groups, and they were forthcoming about how many students they were already advising and how much time they could allocate to my research. They also discussed how many hours I needed to work in the lab and commit to group meetings. Some of them described in detail how they would coach me. Others simply said they would assign me to a graduate student who would be in charge of my coaching and training. They also were interested to know about my LSAMP funding—the stipend that the lab and I would receive for my work as an undergraduate researcher, which meant that they would not have to use any money from their research budgets to support me in their lab.

Each of the professors I met with reacted to me very positively. But which one would be the best for me to work with? These interviews left me feeling a little dizzy and unclear about how to make my decision. There seemed to be so much to consider.

A Bud Opens: Finding My First Advisor

Finally, after talking to four professors who, despite their congeniality, did not seem like the best fit for my research interests, I found one that I really clicked with. Dr. María Gutiérrez did things a little differently than the others. In a word, she was organized. Instead of one-to-one appointments for these interviews, she set up a meeting in a conference room and invited four other undergraduate students interested in doing research to attend. She also included four of her graduate students in this meeting. And, she had an agenda for the meeting projected on a screen, which we could easily follow. I could see from her agenda that I wouldn't need my Internet profile or my list of questions. First came the introductions. She introduced herself and then asked us to introduce ourselves to the group. She started her presentation with a description of her research agenda and her major career accomplishments. I liked the way she talked about research and also that she had invited her own graduate students to attend the meeting.

The bullet points on her agenda included a brief introduction to the various projects in which each of the different graduate students were engaged. She told us that each undergraduate student would be trained by one of her graduate students. The graduate students then summarized their research projects and explained how they would help us acclimate to the research group if we decided to join. Each of the research projects had clear goals and well-defined stages with clear objectives, techniques used, and reactions performed. The goals for each project were project dependent, but each one fit with the others thematically like a piece in a big puzzle. Dr. Gutiérrez also mentioned that if we joined her group, we would be able to work independently and on our own "in no time."

The graduate students all said that they would accept undergraduate students as mentees, and jokingly, as "free labor." The mood among them was professional, but friendly. They shared not only information about their research projects but also insights on the research each group did in general. This sharing was interesting and appealing. None of them acted as if they were required to be there. Plus they said they often traveled to give research presentations at conferences. They also explained that the work in the lab was difficult, and that many hours of hard work went into obtaining results. In the end though, they seemed to enjoy their work and this way of life.

Dr. Gutiérrez's well-organized approach to her lab made it possible for students to divide the research into smaller, doable tasks so that each person could find a definite place to contribute to the overall lab research agenda. The picture they painted motivated me to be one of them, to be part of that group. Moreover, these graduate students seemed to like Dr. Gutiérrez. As a person she seemed to be a very interesting and passionate researcher. Her tone of voice was calm, but at the same time it had a hint of excitement. She sounded inspired by her work and had an enthusiasm that also motivated me. Her approach and communication style were very clear and straightforward, not overly friendly, which was different from the other faculty mentors I had interviewed. She spoke from her knowledge and convictions. Her excitement about her research, her good organization, and her inclusion of her graduate students in this meeting appealed to me, and inspired me to make the decision to join her group.

Given all of the positive aspects of her lab, after the meeting I told her I thought she would be the best mentor for me, but I still had one more professor to interview on my list. Dr. Gutiérrez was very positive and told me to take my time in making up my mind. I felt very strange, because I knew I wanted to join her group—but I thought I still had better honor my appointment with the last professor on my list, Dr. Prado-Gómez. I didn't want to cancel my appointment with him fifteen minutes before I was supposed to meet him, even though I was sure I would join Dr. Gutiérrez's lab.

So off I went to Dr. Prado-Gómez's office. One look inside and I knew right away that this professor was not going to work out for me. His office looked like hurricane San Felipe had just hit: a big mess. The extra chair in his office had to be cleared of papers before I could even sit down. Even so, Professor Prado-Gómez was very friendly and interested in my studies and very easy to talk with. I actually liked him and wavered in my decision for a minute. His research sounded interesting, but he said he didn't know exactly how I would fit into it. He thought that we could work this out as we went along. His lack of a well-defined job description was a red flag. I was relieved to know that Dr. Gutiérrez and her graduate students were there as an alternative. I had heard horror stories about students getting into lab situations that were ill-defined and in which the work they were to do was not clearly set out for them from the beginning. These labs were often full of strife and conflict as a result, no matter how friendly the professor was.

Our conversation started to ramble so I reverted to my little set of questions, which he cordially answered. I was polite, but when I left I practically ran back to Dr. Gutiérrez and her students. I went straight to her office and told her I definitely wanted her for my undergraduate research advisor. She said she would accept me as part of her research group, and I nearly jumped up out of my chair with happy relief. I shook her hand, and then went to find my friend to tell her about my success.

A Healthy Garden Makes for Strong Trees

I started working in Dr. Gutiérrez's lab that summer. As she had promised us, after a year or so of training with our respective graduate mentors, we were able to work independently on parts of the lab's research projects. Eventually, as an undergraduate senior, I also trained and mentored other undergraduate students in the basic techniques used in the lab. As Dr. Gutiérrez had shown me, I prepared research agendas for every meeting in the lab and ensured that we had a list of things to do for each day of the week. My freshman and sophomore mentees were able to present their research at various local conferences, and I had the opportunity to be a coauthor of their research papers. I saw this opportunity as another step toward my goal of getting a PhD and becoming a faculty member.

During the time that I worked in Dr. Gutiérrez's lab I felt that I was part of a group and was comfortable with what I was achieving as an undergraduate researcher. Then I started asking myself, What will I do after graduation? Do I really want to follow through and go to graduate school? Am I good at this? Do I truly want to be a professor or a researcher? The answer to all of these questions was *yes*. I would be brave and seek out my future as a research chemist. As for choosing a graduate advisor, the choice was already made. I never had a question as to who would be my advisor for my MS degree. I fully trusted Dr. Gutiérrez and respected her as a research scientist and as a mentor. I felt that I belonged there in her lab. I spoke with Dr. Gutiérrez and told her that I wanted to continue graduate studies with the project I was working on, and I asked her to be my major advisor. She enthusiastically supported this plan. The semester before graduation, I applied to graduate school at the UPR–Mayagüez campus and was accepted into the graduate program in chemistry.

The capstone of my undergraduate years came when my whole family watched me graduate and receive my bachelor of science diploma. As we were leaving the auditorium Dr. Gutiérrez came over to me and I introduced her to my family. She congratulated me and gave me a big hug. I knew that I was taking a big step in my life—the beginning of a new journey. I was moving on to my graduate studies. Graduation was only a symbolic event, however, because I was staying at the same university and continuing with my research in Dr. Gutiérrez's lab. Nevertheless, I was turning a page in my biography as a student and as a researcher.

Bloom Where You Are Planted

Throughout my master's degree program, I was grateful to have Dr. Gutiérrez as my mentor. The project I had started the year before involved a search for compounds that had a reactivity similar to that of cisplatin, a drug used to treat certain cancers. We learned that some of these compounds have varying levels of response to in vitro cancer cells. Although many more studies would be needed before these drugs could be used to help cancer patients, I felt that I was contributing to the chemistry world and to cancer research.

Dr. Gutiérrez was also an excellent professor. I took three courses with her: Inorganic Chemistry, Advanced Inorganic Chemistry, and Methods and Techniques of Inorganic Chemistry at the Micro Scale. I did very well in all of these, but taken together with the lab work and teaching, it was a lot of pressure and I had to study very hard.

During my years as a graduate student working with Dr. Gutiérrez, I accomplished many of my research goals. Then I was introduced to another instrumental technique, surface-enhanced Raman spectroscopy, and I started working with a colleague of Dr. Gutiérrez and collaborated with her research group. Although productive, those years were tough. I had to balance this interdisciplinary research project with my coursework, my teaching assistant duties at the university, and my job as a high school chemistry teacher. I also had undergraduate students under my supervision in the lab that I had to mentor. Plus, I was a lab instructor for organic chemistry for chemistry majors, and this lab required a lot of preparation. I had to attend many staff meetings and reagent preparation meetings for it because I participated in the lecture portion of the course. I also helped grade the course exams. Throughout all of this, Dr. Gutiérrez remained my steady rock on whom I could depend and who guided me when I encountered difficulties in my teaching and research.

Sometimes the Apple Falls a Little Far from the Tree

During my master's program at UPR–Mayagüez, I had the good fortune to be selected for a GK-12 fellowship. I did not know at the time that this experience would open a completely new door for me as a teacher, researcher, and scholar. As a fellow participating in this research grant, I was able to bring my science knowledge to a middle school science classroom. I was very curious to see how the middle school students would react when I presented science concepts to them and was pleased to learn that they really liked learning about science. I then participated in several professional development workshops that focused on discipline-based education research. I had never imagined that this type of educational research was possible and could be so interesting. It really inspired me, and I started to think that I might want to pursue it at the PhD level. So, I put together an abstract for a paper at a chemical education conference that was going to be held at UPR–San Juan. It was accepted and off I went to this conference. Little did I know that I would have two encounters there that would change the course of my life and carry me very far away from my enchanted island home.

The first important encounter happened in my conference session. Another chemistry major from UPR–Mayagüez, Kermin Hernández, was presenting a paper. We had met before at department functions, but we had never really had a conversation or gotten to know each other. We had time at this conference to go to lunch, and it was then that I knew another new and significant phase in my life was beginning.

The second meeting that changed my life occurred when I spoke with the principal investigator of the GK-12 fellowship, who was also at this conference. We discussed the highly interesting field of educational research in the field of chemical education. I asked her which university had the best chemical education program, and she recommended Purdue University, commenting that it had *the* pioneer program in chemical education studies. I was a little taken aback. Graduate school was difficult enough in my own country and my own language. Sure, everyone could say, "Hi, how's it going?" in English, but could I read and write at the research level in English in the field of chemical education, and could I function while living far away from my family and my beloved Dr. Gutiérrez? I was not sure I could do it.

Back at UPR–Mayagüez, my newfound friendship with Kermin developed into a serious romance, and after not too long, we decided to get married. Since we had the same career goals in chemical education, and both of us had been directed to Purdue University in West Lafayette, Indiana, we decided to move there after completing our master's degrees. I decided that I would pursue chemical education at the master's degree level, perfect my English during this second master's program, and then go on to the PhD. So, I took the GK-12 fellowship principal investigator up on his recommendation of Purdue's excellent chemical education program. I applied to the Master of Science in Education program in the Department of Curriculum & Instruction (C&I) at Purdue and was accepted.

UPR–Mayagüez was still my academic home, however, where I had to finish up my MS in chemistry program with Dr. Gutiérrez. Although she was very happy for me that I had been accepted into the chemical education program at Purdue, neither of us liked the idea that I would fulfill my dream of earning my PhD in a place so far away. More than my primary advisor, she was the center of my life as a researcher, and I had become one of her best and most reliable students. We resolved to keep in touch, and that I would stop by and see her whenever I was home for a visit. Otherwise, all she could do was give me her blessing and send me on my way, and all I could do was give her a big hug and say, "Thank you."

Falling in Love Is a Breeze; Falling from a Tree Can Be Painful

Anyone who has been through the last semester of a master's program will tell you how hectic and busy everything is. Being in love and planning your wedding on top of this graduation process leads to an exceptionally hectic and busy life. I say this because, unlike Kermin, I just trusted that everything would work out at Purdue once I got there, and I didn't remove the stars from my eyes to get a clear look at the advisor situation at Purdue before I arrived. I said goodbye to Puerto Rico and Dr. Gutiérrez much like Dorothy said farewell to Oz when she clicked her heels together and the good fairy sent her on her way. Unfortunately, I was in for some surprises when it came time to choose my master's thesis advisor at Purdue, circumstances which could have been avoided if I would have been better at asking questions before I moved there. Similar to Dorothy, I did eventually wake up in a safe and comfortable place, but with a few ounces of prevention, I might have avoided a pretty severe bruise on my academic heart.

The Harsh Wind That Blew

In the midst of unpacking the meager possessions we brought from Puerto Rico, I started my first semester in graduate school at Purdue. I enrolled in education and chemistry courses that were very interesting and I really liked them: Survey in Science Education and Chemistry and Advanced Mass Spectroscopy. Then, the romantic stars in my eyes began to give way to clear eyesight in terms of finding my thesis advisor at Purdue. First, I learned during the orientation week that in Purdue's C&I department, the procedures for choosing a thesis advisor are quite different from those in the Department of Chemistry, which Kermin had investigated before applying to Purdue. In C&I, the department assigns a faculty advisor to each master's student when he or she is accepted into the graduate program.

A week before school started, I received a departmental e-mail informing me that I had been assigned to the lab of Dr. James Jannis. Since I did not know Dr. Jannis or his research interests, the first thing I did was to look him up on the C&I department website, where I found a link to his web page. I was able to read about his research interests and gain valuable information about the type of research his students were conducting. A list of Dr. Jannis's recent publications was included on the website as well, and I selected two to read. The publications gave me an idea of what kind of projects he was interested in and an overview of his group's research agenda. Once I finished reading these articles, I decided to e-mail him, introduce myself, and set up an appointment. He immediately responded to my e-mail and we set up an appointment for the following week.

For that whole week I was rather stressed because I didn't know what questions he would ask me at our meeting. I had an extensive list of questions that I wanted to ask him, but I didn't know how he would react to them. Most of all, I didn't want to appear naïve about the whole graduate school process at Purdue. I felt like I was back at the beginning of my undergraduate program. Finally, the date of the appointment came, and I went to meet him at his office. The door was open, and I looked in and saw that his office was huge. It had big, tall, and old windows, reminiscent of home. Dr. Jannis was at his computer. He asked me to come in; however, he didn't look at me at all. I introduced myself and remained standing for a couple of minutes. Eventually, I decided to sit down, since he didn't offer me a chair.

I sat there patiently waiting for him and, after a few minutes, he finished reading his e-mails and then turned around to talk to me. The first thing he asked me to do was to look at the departmental, College of Education, and Graduate School websites and familiarize myself with them, something I had already done. However, I didn't tell him this because I didn't want to sound knowledgeable and have him ask me questions that I would be unable to answer. I made a mental note to go through the websites one more time to make sure I had understood them. Second, he asked me to come up with a list of research questions related to a particular topic he gave me. I looked at him in shock. Wasn't I going to be able to select my own research project? It seemed like the answer to this question was no. Apparently, he had something else in mind. He was giving me the research topic; I just had to develop it. Third, he asked me to set up weekly individual meetings with him to discuss my research project progress. At this moment, I mentally hit the brakes. *What?* I didn't know where to begin with the topic he had given me. I hadn't even started an educational research course yet, or any course related to the discipline for that matter. My master's degree was in inorganic chemistry, where I had done mostly wet lab and bench work. What was he saying?

I just hid my anxiety and nervousness and pretended to understand what he was talking about and tried to memorize every single methodological term he mentioned as he said it. I also took some notes so that I could refresh my memory when I looked it all up later.

Finally, he took me to his lab, showed me my desk, and introduced me to the graduate student lab crew: Elena from Honduras, Adelet from Turkey, and Melvin from Texas. Apparently more graduate students were in the group, but they were in the process of dissertating and were working from home, so I couldn't meet them that day. After these hellos, I immediately began setting up my workspace and went to get my office and building keys. Despite Dr. Jannis's rather cold demeanor, at that point in time I felt like I was going to fit into this group. They all treated me well and seemed very courteous. The Honduran student was very nice and she spoke Spanish, which made me feel accepted. It was, however, all so sudden and strange. But what could I do? There was no leaving and going back to the safety of the lab with Dr. Gutiérrez, even though nothing seemed more appealing to me at that moment.

Even though I felt more or less welcome in Dr. Jannis's research group, he did not know me at all, and my research interests did not align with his research agenda. This discrepancy between our interests didn't seem important to him, though. Despite this mismatch, the first couple of months were very interesting, and I got to know my new advisor a little better and made friends with the group in his lab. I tried to do everything that he asked me to do, but as time went by, I started to feel a little bit intimidated. He had more than occasional mood swings, and I really didn't know how or when to approach him. Every time I started some new project, he rejected it, and I had to start all over again. I fully understood the research process, but he was not approachable. When I thought that I was on the right track, he would say that I had to change the topic or research approach one more time.

I could not believe he was treating me like this. After all of my successes from a very early age, and all that I had learned and been responsible for in Dr. Gutiérrez's lab, Dr. Jannis's behavior toward me seemed absolutely bizarre, as if he had just landed from another planet and had no idea what was going on around him. Over the period of the first year and a half, our lack of communication escalated, and eventually it was impossible to have any honest and open verbal exchange with him. The others in the lab had similar difficulties with him, but theirs were less intense than mine. I definitely felt like the scapegoat of the group. I tried multiple times to approach him to talk about these difficulties, but without any success. The situation was intolerable to the point that for the first time in my life, I thought about quitting graduate school.

I decided to contact a couple of people to try to find a solution to my problem before giving up on my dreams. I thought about Dr. Gutiérrez and knew that she would not want me to let this person get in my way like this. Two of my good friends suggested that I go and talk to two professors in another department about my problem. I contacted them both and set up appointments. Initially I didn't know if talking with them was a good idea, but I felt that I didn't have any other option. I didn't feel comfortable or secure talking with the head of my home department because I really didn't want him to know that I was having these problems and then talk with my advisor about me. However, my friends assured me that these professors were very friendly and trustworthy, so I decided to meet with them to try to find some comfort and someone who could help me.

I shared my story with the two professors, and in both meetings we talked for an hour or more. Surprisingly, both of them gave me the exact same advice: that I talk openly and honestly with my advisor about what was working for me and what wasn't, and how we might improve our communication.

The Plant Uprooted . . .

I took these professors' advice, and during my next individual meeting with my advisor, I approached him and asked if we could talk about the problems I was having. As my confidants had advised, I approached the situation as if my problems were causing the difficulties—as if I was the one who didn't have good communication skills, and I wanted to improve this aspect of our advisor–graduate student relationship. I had rehearsed what I wanted to say multiple times, but the outcome of this conversation was nevertheless unexpected. He did not respond well to the conversation. In fact, he became very agitated. I had experienced his mood swings for almost two years, but I had never seen him as angry as he was that day. He shouted and said that I should consider leaving the research group and find someone else to work with.

His extremely emotional and verbally violent response to my question took me by surprise, and even though I tried not to cry, once the first tear ran down my cheek, I couldn't stop. I was a complete mess. Even so, I looked him straight in the eyes through my tears, then excused myself and ran to the restroom down the hall. That encounter remains with me as one of the most embarrassing moments of my life. I have always been very strong in my decisions, and never in a million years would I imagine that I would react the way I did that afternoon. I couldn't help but think about Dr. Gutiérrez and how differently she would have responded to me in this situation, not to mention how much I missed her.

After a couple of minutes in the restroom I calmed down. I immediately called my husband and told him what had happened. I was just devastated and thought that I was going to lose my place in the C&I graduate program. My husband helped me to realize that Purdue had other people and support offices that I could approach to try to find a solution to my problem. He told me that even if I didn't have an advisor at this moment, I was still in graduate school and my scholarly performance was good. I had always followed all of the guidelines and requirements of my program. I started to feel a little better, but I didn't want to go back to my desk in the lab for fear of seeing Elena and falling apart again. So I simply left the building and went home.

It took me a couple of days to realize that I had been asked to leave the research group and that I had to find a new advisor whose research interests were a better match with mine. If it hadn't been for the interesting coursework, I don't think I would have been able to cope. But the courses were very good, and I was learning a great deal about the field of chemistry education, which I was more and more interested in with every paper that I researched and wrote. So, this work kept me afloat and functional despite my lab situation, even though it was hard to tolerate. I spent most of my time outside of class at home. I knew I needed to snap out of my doldrums and do something about my advisor situation, but I was slow to act for fear of a repeat of what I had encountered with Dr. Jannis.

One morning, however, I woke up and just told myself to do something about my problem and stop hiding in my room. Images of all of my achievements came into my mind: my ingenious hydroponic plants project, the way I managed Dr. Gutiérrez's lab, my stellar teaching evaluations, and all of the papers I had presented at major conferences in my field. Who did Dr. Jannis think he was that he could try to keep me down like this? I went straight to my computer, e-mailed the chair of my department, and requested an appointment. A couple of days later I was in his office discussing my situation and I discovered that my husband was completely right. Although I had been asked to leave a research group, I was still in graduate school, and I just needed to find a new advisor.

This meeting gave me some hope and strengthened my belief that I could find someone who would accept me in his or her lab. I figured I had gone through the search for an advisor before, and I could do it again. I didn't waste any more time. I e-mailed every professor individually who was part of the science education division in C&I and chemistry. I set up appointments and met with the majority of them, and I asked each one if I could join his or her research group. Some of them already knew that I had been asked to find a new advisor. Either Dr. Jannis had given them a bad report on me, or since I had met with so many professors, they had already talked with each other about my situation.

At the beginning of my search I felt uncomfortable explaining what had happened and asking these professors if I could join their group. This experience was overwhelming, because instead of preparing myself to meet one advisor, I had to prepare my story and meet ten possible advisors. Nevertheless, I went to each professor's website and read at least one of his or her major publications. I made cheat sheets with key points about each professor's research interests, and the ways my interests would fit with the lab groups. I was exhausted and tired of trying to fit in. I needed to sound professional, and somehow communicate that it was not entirely my fault that I needed to find a new advisor. However, I didn't want to attack or speak ill of Dr. Jannis. I just wanted to find a new professor with whom I could work and who would appreciate me and value my research knowledge and lab skills.

Transplant Successful

Fortunately that semester I was taking a graduate course titled Topics in Chemical Education, taught by Dr. Moreland. She had selected a list of topics that covered the most recent research in this emerging field. Her course provided an overview of the literature in each of the areas of chemical education, including chemistry misconceptions and conceptual change, as well as theories of learning from Piaget and Vygotsky to radical constructivism, distributed cognition, and developing and assessing instructional materials. I did well in her course and I developed a great respect for Dr. Moreland's mastery of her field and respectful treatment of her graduate students. After grades were in and everything had calmed down at the end of the spring semester, I decided to set up a meeting with her, which was one of my last "advisor search" appointments. By this time, the end of the semester, Dr. Moreland had gotten to know me as a student, and she was concerned when I told her about my advisor situation. She listened to my story and said that she would be interested in having me in her lab group. I nearly teared up with gratitude. She was very courteous and we immediately started talking about my interests beyond chemistry research. She wanted to know me for who I was, not just as an extension of her own research interests. We talked for hours about both of our travels, interests in chemistry research, research group experiences, and my good performance in her class.

I felt deeply grateful when she offered to show me her lab and introduce me to her research group, and I sensed immediately that I was welcome there, even though we only stayed long enough for basic introductions. She was open to letting me pursue my own research interests and didn't require her students to follow her research agenda exactly. The feeling was good; I was relaxed and able to talk and ask questions without the pressure of being judged or criticized all the time. I felt that her interests meshed with mine. She was a very good instructor, and I could work with her much more productively than I could with Dr. Jannis, with whom I had not chosen to work in the first place. Even so, I didn't make my decision to join her group right away. I needed some time to think about what I wanted to do and reflect on my other advisor interviews. I knew though, deep inside me, that she was the one with whom I really wanted to work. But as always, I came home and sat down to record the pros and cons of all my meetings. I assigned value numbers to each one. After sleeping for a night on my pros and cons list, I woke up and decided to follow my gut—I would choose Dr. Moreland as my new advisor.

Even though I had decided on Dr. Moreland and I had met the graduate students in her lab, this time I was not going to make the same mistake as before and get into a lab that I knew nothing about. I looked up the graduate students in her lab on the web, and then went and talked to them in the lab. Since I had only been there for a few minutes the first time, I now wanted to look carefully and see what it was really like in that lab. Was it in fact organized, or depressing, or cheerful? My experience during that visit affirmed my sense that Dr. Moreland was the person I wanted for my advisor. Her lab was organized and up to speed. I decided to join her research group and e-mailed her to inform her of my decision. She responded that she was very happy to have me join her group. After breathing a significant sigh of relief, the next step was to start the process of actually changing advisors on paper.

I went to the College of Education graduate office and they explained the procedure for changing advisors. I needed to complete paperwork downloadable from the College of Education's website and submit it to the graduate office. I printed out the forms I needed. Much to my frustration, changing advisors was more involved than I had anticipated. I needed to obtain what seemed like an endless number of signatures: the new advisor, the former advisor, the department head, and the graduate school director. All needed to sign the forms before they could be sent to the Purdue Graduate School for final processing.

Unfortunately for me, this meant I had to meet with Dr. Jannis one more time before I could officially switch research groups. He not only had to sign some of the forms, but he also had to state the reasons I was leaving his lab. I thought that all of this red tape was pointless and oppressive. Having to deal with Dr. Jannis again made me feel very uncomfortable. It would be a nerve-wracking experience. I really didn't want to talk to him or even look at him, but I also knew that fear and hesitation would only make things worse. The only way to move on from this experience was to bravely confront reality. I summoned up the courage to go to his office for his signature, but even though I wanted to be more specific, I was unable to express, or I didn't feel comfortable stating in words on the form, exactly why I was leaving the research group. I invented a superficial excuse that didn't clearly state the real reasons for my switch. He was not so happy with my statement on the form, but he finally decided to sign it. Hallelujah! I was free, and at last able to move on with my graduate career and the fulfillment of my dreams.

The following fall semester I was an official member of Dr. Moreland's research group. She turned out to be a very good advisor, much like Dr. Gutiérrez. She asked me to write a research prospectus addressing my research interests and the goals I would like to achieve with my master's thesis. We set up regular individual meetings so I could discuss my progress on my research prospectus. Although it wasn't due until the end of the fall semester, I had my prospectus done in less than two months. I also submitted all the paperwork to the Institutional Review Board for review and approval to conduct my research in the high school setting. I was fully ready to work on my thesis project. By the end of the fall semester I was collecting data. By the end of the following spring semester the pilot studies were completed. Dr. Moreland was very helpful and gave good suggestions on ways to address my research methodology, analyze my data, and write my thesis. Two years later with her as my advisor, I completed my second master's degree, this one in education.

Blessed Are the Advisors Who Water Their Indoor Plants

My Purdue adventure didn't stop there, however. Based on my positive experience with Dr. Moreland as my master's thesis advisor, I decided to go on and pursue a PhD degree in chemistry education under her guidance and mentorship. This time, I knew exactly what I was getting into. I was confident that my goals and expectations meshed with hers, and that the challenges of pursuing a PhD would not be complicated by difficulties incurred due to a bad fit with my advisor. I applied to Purdue's PhD program in chemistry education and was accepted. I can imagine that if my master's thesis advisor experience had not been as good as mine had been with Dr. Moreland, I might not have gone on to the PhD level. Her good advising clearly inspired me to pursue the PhD. Given that I had worked with her so successfully during my master's degree program, Dr. Moreland was the obvious choice for my PhD advisor.

In the final year of my PhD program, Dr. Moreland proved again that she was an excellent advisor and provided opportunities for my growth as a researcher and scholar in the field of chemical education. She was very interested in and supportive of my thesis topic, "Examining the Effects of Laboratory Instruction on High School Chemistry Students' Conceptual Understanding of Chemical Equilibrium." Her encouragement and support of my interests has been very important to me, and I think that such a positive attitude toward one's students is essential in an advisor. I was able to engage in the research topic that interested me and that I was passionate about investigating. In addition, she allowed me to conduct research studies different from but related to my dissertation and encouraged me to explore other research interests in order to expand my research skills and portfolio. Taken together, she opened the doors to a very gratifying experience in my chosen field and a successful career in chemical education.

In the spring of my fifth year of graduate school at Purdue, I received my PhD in curriculum and instruction—chemistry education, and in many ways, this success was due to my choice of thesis advisor. If I hadn't had the courage to make the change that I knew I needed to make during my master's program, I might not have been able to work with Dr. Moreland and have such a positive outcome with my PhD degree. Losing two years, weighed against what I gained by finding my new advisor, completing my PhD degree in three years, and most important, discovering a field that I love and am fully committed to working in for the rest of my career, was completely worth the struggle. Also, it's hard to say how much my positive experience with undergraduate research also contributed to my current sense of mastery in my field. I know my research and technical abilities were greatly strengthened through my work in Dr. Gutiérrez's lab back in UPR–Mayagüez, and this work definitely helped boost my confidence and motivation to continue along the difficult pathway I encountered during my master's degree program.

Good Soil, Good Fruit

All of the outcomes of these experiences prove that the consequences of the thesis advisor choice are very real and long lasting. Standing your ground and going for the thing you want most remains the name of the game in graduate professional development. My chosen research advisors provided me with the academic, professional, and personal support I needed throughout my graduate career. Their advice and guidance have been invaluable, and I know I will try to follow their examples with my future students.

CONCLUSION

As much as possible, know what you are getting into before you start a graduate program. And once you are there, don't be afraid to make the changes you need to make to ensure that your program meets your needs and interests. Providing positive support is the hallmark of a good advisor. As a graduate student dedicating your life to a field of study, you deserve healthy, mutually beneficial communication and interaction with your major advisor. Make sure you check the who's who of your department to avoid choosing someone who won't give you the support you'll need. I am happy and proud to say that I successfully traveled through the forest of graduate school and completed my PhD. I now am looking forward to my new job as an adjunct faculty member in the field of chemistry education at a great liberal arts college in upstate New York.

CHAPTER 4 GROUP DISCUSSION

As Nahyr's story illustrates, the advisor–graduate student relationship can present unexpected challenges, and navigating a successful advisor change requires forbearance and diplomacy. Because of her perseverance and strong belief in herself, Nahyr was able to make this change. Looking back on her experience, she now can say that she not only made it through this difficult process successfully, but she also learned from it.

The chapter 4 video, titled *Reflections*, continues the saga from the chapter 3 video, *The Move*. In *The Move*, Professor Harrison's graduate students were confronted with his unexpected relocation to another university. In *Reflections*, we meet these same students a few months later and learn how they dealt with the transition. The discussion activity following this video gives you a chance to experiment with reflective learning that will support your success as you move through your PhD program. The video and accompanying materials for leading a group discussion on this chapter can be downloaded from the chapter 4 resource web page at http://dx.doi.org/10.5703/1288284315201.

CHAPTER AUTHOR PROFILE

Nahyr D. Rovira-Figueroa, PhD

Dr. Rovira-Figueroa is from Puerto Rico, the island of enchantment. She has BS and MS degrees in chemistry from the University of Puerto Rico–Mayagüez as well as a teacher licensure in high school chemistry. Dr. Rovira-Figueroa earned her MS in education and her PhD in science education from Purdue University. During her graduate student career, she presented research papers at many national and regional professional meetings and received the Outstanding Oral Presentation Award at the 2008 National Society for the Advancement of Chicanos and Native Americans in Science (SACNAS)

Conference. She has been awarded several grants for outreach projects to disadvantaged schools in the Greater Lafayette Area Latino Community. During the summer of 2012, Dr. Rovira-Figueroa worked as a visiting associate lecturer for the Engineering Summer Program at the University of Wisconsin–Madison. She is currently an adjunct faculty professor and general chemistry coordinator for the Chemistry Department at St. John Fisher College and adjunct lecturer for the Ella Cline Shear School of Education at State University of New York–Geneseo Campus.

Chapter 5

Working with Committee Members

Charles M. Rubert Pérez, PhD

⬅—————————————————————➡

INTRODUCTION

Usually by the time graduate students reach the second year of their PhD program, they have completed most of their coursework, started their research, and are thinking about their thesis proposal, preliminary exams, publishing papers, and presenting at conferences. From this point forward, graduate students work on research under their advisor until graduation, and therefore a good student/advisor relationship is imperative for success. But also important is the composition of the graduate committee. After all, apart from the research advisor, the graduate committee has the most influence on yearly evaluations, the thesis project, and the final degree approval. Committee members can sometimes seem intimidating, and having a professional and amicable relationship with them can be very helpful. The well-chosen committee can provide support and guidance to keep a student on the right track to graduate in a timely fashion.

This chapter relates some of my experiences in creating and maintaining good relationships with my advisor and committee members. In it I offer tips on how to efficiently select a good committee and how to prepare materials for them. I also share some of my personal stories about selecting an advisor and committee members in order to make this process more tangible for those who will soon be in the process of selecting their own committee. Hopefully, this chapter will give you some insight into how to work constructively with your graduate committee members.

SELECTING YOUR COMMITTEE

Whether you have just finished your first year or you're at the end of your second year, eventually you will select a committee to review and evaluate your work. Committee members are usually professors with whom you have some type of connection. You may choose a professor who taught a graduate level course that you enjoyed, one you worked under as a teaching assistant, or one with whom you are currently collaborating. Or you might choose a mentor who has guided you in your studies.

My entrance into my PhD work was unusual in that during my first year I switched from the biology department to the chemistry department. Because of this, my approach to selecting committee members was also a little unusual. When I started my graduate program, I was accepted into the biology department to do research in the area of biochemistry, which was a new area of study for me. As an eager first-year graduate student, I was excited to start taking classes and learn more complicated things about proteins and DNA than I had covered as an undergraduate. I was also curious and motivated to start doing rotations and learn new techniques and skills. However, after only two months my excitement started to fade. Call me impatient, but I quickly realized that I did not find the research in the department very interesting or motivating. The classes I was taking were not providing an environment in which I felt I could excel. All the students in my classes seemed to be well adjusted and enjoying the coursework and research, but I felt a little bit uneasy. I remember thinking, Is this what graduate school is supposed to feel like? I really liked learning about biochemistry as an undergraduate, but I wondered if this field was really for me. Maybe I made a risky move trying to actually do biochemical research; it looked so different in the books than from the bench. One thing I knew for sure: I was not happy.

In that moment of insecurity, I contemplated my options: do I continue in this department for another year and see if I learn to like it, do I move to the chemistry department where there's biochemistry research as well, or do I quit graduate school and start all over again? The first option seemed like it would just prolong the problem and the last option seemed too extreme given that I had just started graduate school. So I chose the remaining option: I decided to change departments. It may have been a rash decision not to give the biology department another chance, but my gut feeling said to move to the chemistry department, and that's what I did.

In order to change departments, I had to submit my application to the chemistry department to see if I was eligible for the chemistry program. I also had to get a form that needed to be signed by the head of the biology department allowing me to keep my graduate student status while I reapplied to graduate school, and this was just the beginning of the red tape. It was not an easy process. In the meantime, I signed up to take yet another class. I wanted a class offered by the chemistry department so I could start to catch up with that program. I was taking too many classes, doing rotations, and dealing with the process of changing departments, as well as getting used to the weather, the language, and the culture in the United States. Stressful, right? Nevertheless, I survived, and despite all of the pressures on me, the chemistry department indeed accepted me into the PhD program for the spring semester.

Because my entry into a new department and program had been so rocky, I wanted to make sure I started off on the right foot in the spring, which meant choosing the right committee. To begin, I needed to choose a research advisor as quickly as I could. I wanted to keep pace with my new classmates, who were already a semester ahead of me. To make up for the lost semester, I took some time to research my professors online as well as visit the labs of professors whose research I found interesting. I put together a list of eight professors whose research fit my interests and e-mailed them to set up individual meetings with them. In preparing for these conversations, I tried to think of appropriate questions: What type of research projects do you do? What will be expected from me as your student? What skills will I develop from this training? And so on.

I remember nervously knocking on one professor's door for one of my meetings. The professor greeted me with a welcoming voice and right away I started to feel more relaxed. After that, it was down to business. He sat down behind his desk and we were looking at one another face-to-face. He then positioned the monitor of his computer so I could see it and started to go through a PowerPoint presentation that summarized his research. He gave me a good overview of his projects. He spoke with excitement and clearly explained the importance of his work. When it comes to recruiting new students, some professors have the ability to draw you in so well they put even the best telemarketer to shame. He was one of those professors. As I listened to the presentation, I thought of possible questions regarding the aspects of his research that I liked. After a small discussion, I shared some details about my past research experiences and my future goals so he could better get to know my professional interests. He seemed interested in my project ideas and I had a good feeling about the conversation with him. After this meeting I stepped out of his office and made a mental note of the things I liked and did not like about his research, then continued on my way to prepare for my next meeting.

I consider myself to be somewhat of a shy person, but one thing graduate school has taught me is to reach out to my peers. You can learn a great deal by talking to fellow graduate students. So in addition to my meetings, I asked other graduate students their opinions of the different professors on my list to help me decide which lab to join. I was looking for genuine and sincere answers. After all, I did not want to change departments again or leave graduate school after everything I'd been through. After going through this lengthy meeting process and taking my peers' suggestions into account, I narrowed my list and had a final talk with the professor who I hoped would be my advisor.

As I was walking to my soon-to-be advisor's office to tell her I would like to have her as my advisor, I was excited but nervous at the same time. I wasn't sure if another graduate student might have taken the last open position in her lab. If that had happened, I guess I could have considered my second or third choice, so it wouldn't have been the end of the world. But for a split second, it felt like it would have been exactly that. Taking a few deep breaths, I regained a positive attitude. There was her office in front of me. I knocked. She opened the door and greeted me enthusiastically. All my worries faded away once she said she would be happy if I joined her group. We started talking about research topics, and she gave me some reading materials on each of the projects she was overseeing in her lab. She helped me decide which project group I wanted to join. By that afternoon, I had a desk and a hood and at last I could settle into a lab after being a nomad in the department for several weeks. I felt very comfortable with my choice, which also reaffirmed my decision to move to a new department despite the hard work it had required.

Thanks to this experience, two years later when it came time to select the rest of my committee members, instead of feeling like I was behind, I actually felt way ahead. I already had a list of professors whose research I knew fit my interests, as well as an approach for selecting professors that I knew would allow me to make the best decisions. The PhD committee in my department consists of three faculty members (the major professor and two department faculty) who evaluate the first two years of work. In my case, this included my lab research, preliminary exams, and research proposal. So I got to work and made a list of possible choices for my committee, just as I had done when selecting my advisor. And again, I asked fellow students for their opinions and input on this matter. My list consisted primarily of professors I had met when I first joined the biology department, as well as professors I had taken classes from during my first two years in the chemistry department. One of the chemistry professors on my list I had collaborated with on a research project. My fellow graduate students pointed me toward professors who would give constructive criticism, so I could make good progress on my research.

After narrowing down my choices, I went to consult with my advisor, since I really valued her opinion. I wanted to make sure she agreed with my choices to assure there would be good "chemistry," no pun intended, between all my committee members during my preliminary exams and subsequent work with them on my thesis project. This time I was pretty comfortable as I stepped into her office with my little yellow notebook containing the names of the prospective committee members I had identified. After almost two years of working in her research lab, I had a good professional relationship with her and felt comfortable discussing my ideas and future goals. She opened the office door with her tea in hand and invited me in. She listened as I went down my list. I had to pick two. We discussed the reasons I had chosen the people I did. At the time, I was working on a project that was part of a collaboration with another lab, so I definitely wanted to include the professor overseeing the other lab because we had interacted various times already to talk about research. My advisor agreed, which left one more person I had to choose. The other people on my list were mostly professors who taught classes in which I had done well, a couple with whom I had briefly interacted to ask for help on certain topics, and a professor simply recommended to me by several graduate students. I decided on one of the professors from whom I had taken a class, and that was it. Thanks to this brief meeting with my advisor, I had my final decision and another checkmark on my graduate school to-do list. Now, I needed to make sure that the two professors I had so painstakingly chosen were available and willing to be part of my committee.

I went and talked to each of the professors to make sure they were able and willing to serve on my committee. Both agreed and with the selection process completed, I submitted my committee list to the department and voilà, I officially had a graduate committee. Now the real fun began. I needed to prepare for my preliminary exams, which consisted of writing a proposal in the format of a National Institutes of Health (NIH) proposal for original research. The topic of my dissertation was not at all related to my lab projects. Keeping both of these going at the same time was a very challenging and daunting task. So I started the demanding but important process of reading and studying different areas of research and trying to think of a new idea in chemistry for my thesis that I would propose to my committee. Apart from reading, I frequently tested my ideas on the more senior graduate students for their feedback. I found these conversations very helpful and would recommend this type of collegial exchange to everybody who is in a similar situation.

It took a couple of months to come up with a good, original idea. Once I had it formulated, I was able to write it up as a research proposal for my committee members. It was challenging, but doable. I just had to stick to the NIH proposal format. Keep in mind that while I was doing all of this, I was also teaching and working on my own research. Two important things that helped me survive were organization and time management. I had to make sure I organized each day so I was able to perform my responsibilities efficiently. Also, I had to give myself time and be prepared for the worst. For example, when I was formulating my proposal idea, I came across literature that contradicted the point I was trying to make, which meant I had to step back and reformulate my position relative to my argument. So, I started my literature review early to allow time early on to address problems that emerged.

After several months of preparation, it was show time. I had submitted my report, after I had revised it a couple of hundred times and had several of my fellow graduate students look it over too, of course. I prepared my presentation and practiced it in front of those who had time to listen, and I studied the material like my life depended on it. I was ready. Or was I? There's always that little bit of doubt lingering in the back of your mind that shows up in situations like this, but there was no turning back. I was absolutely determined and passionately driven to achieve my official PhD candidacy. I still would have to pass my doctoral exams, but that is another story.

When the day of my defense finally arrived, I went to campus an hour early all dressed up for the occasion and headed directly to the room in which I was to present. As I stepped into the rather dark room to set up the projector and my computer, I suddenly felt like I was in one of those dark and not-so-welcoming interrogation rooms they show in the movies when they question the bad guy. Not a good feeling. I turned up the lights and opened the blinds a little, just enough to take the edge off the "interrogation" without causing too much glare on the projection screen. I took a few deep breaths and tried my best to keep my nervousness under control while I finished setting everything up—"Just another presentation," I thought, "I can handle this." I felt myself relax a little. Other than my laptop, I brought a bunch of notes in with me, which would be impossible to consult while presenting, but I brought them anyway as a security blanket. It was as though the papers I had studied and the notes I had taken would be there to take over for me in case I needed to rest in the corner and recuperate for a while after taking a mental beating from my professors.

Bringing myself back to the empty conference room, I sat down and looked at the clock. I still had thirty minutes until everyone arrived. I felt nervous and a little hungry. I remembered I had put a granola bar in my bag the night before just to be prepared and took a few bites. About fifteen minutes later, I heard the voices of my committee members as they were walking down the hall. They came into the conference room one by one with coffee in one hand and a copy of my proposal in the other, smiling and talking among themselves as if nothing too serious was about to happen. They settled comfortably in their chairs as I greeted them and they smiled. My advisor gave an introduction for my presentation and then signaled me to start.

In a slightly trembling voice, I started my presentation. As I warmed up I felt better. I hit my stride and more or less confidently related my proposal idea to the committee. They seemed interested and listened closely to what I was saying, and soon the presentation part of my defense was completed. But then, during the examination phase, my committee did not hold back. Their smiling faces quickly changed to their game faces and the defense was on. For almost an hour, their questions flew at me, and I answered them the best that I could. There were a couple of moments in which interesting discussions emerged between the professors themselves, and I thought they had forgotten about me. However, they soon returned to ask me more questions. I was nervous during the whole process, but I knew I had prepared myself to the best of my ability. I defended my points, listened to their critiques, understood their opinions, and expressed my thoughts. It was very gratifying to see how well the committee worked together and how they became interested in my proposal, giving it a thorough discussion.

After almost an hour of questioning, the final moment had arrived. They asked me to step out of the room so they could make their final decision. I graciously turned and stepped outside into the hallway, and once the door closed behind me, I took a deep breath and rested against the wall. In that moment, I felt like I had just run a marathon and had barely made it. Tired and exhausted, I did my best not to get nervous while I waited. Fortunately after not too long my advisor stepped out of the meeting room with a big smile on her face. She reached out, shook my hand, and said: "Congratulations, you are a PhD candidate." In that moment, I felt massively relieved and extremely glad that all that hard work had paid off.

During the process of my defense, all of my committee members had gotten along well with each other, and their different yet somewhat related research areas led to a rich discussion. They had also given me positive criticism on my proposal and told me how I could improve as a scientist and a researcher. This experience, while it was stressful and time consuming, was a very important—perhaps the most important—learning experience of my graduate career. Who knows if I would have had a less meaningful experience had I not given enough time to the careful choice of my committee?

A key point from my experience is the importance of organization and self-motivation to steer through obstacles. When you get admitted to graduate school, you may be faced with the possibility that things might not work out as well as you had hoped. I quickly realized that the first department I had chosen was not for me, so I decided to find similar research in another department where I felt more comfortable. What at first seemed like a setback in my graduate career became an advantage when I discovered the process that allowed me to select committee members who would mesh and interact well together so I could receive the best feedback possible when discussing my project and completing my research goals.

Although it involves a lot of work, no matter what the situation may be, I advise taking time and carefully considering the type of research you want to conduct when choosing your committee members. After all, most students work with their graduate committee for four to five years, and you want to make sure you are satisfied with your work and the people who are mentoring you through the process. At the same time, you may want to be prepared to choose your committee as early as possible, because other graduate students may also be choosing their committees at the same time, and professors can only be part of a limited number of committees. An important thing to consider is that these people will be there to guide your graduate career and, in the end, they will most likely be the people who write your letters of recommendation for fellowships and future jobs. Thus, you want to be certain you put together a committee that will assist you with your professional and academic needs.

COMMUNICATING WITH YOUR COMMITTEE

Once you are conducting research, the interaction with your committee could be anything from minimal to excessive, depending on your department. For instance, some advisors meet with their graduate students only in group meetings, because many professors travel a lot, are busy writing grants, or are just as busy as their students with their own workload. Other advisors will make it a priority to pass through their students' offices every day to meet with them one on one. Whatever the case, I found that taking the time to plan occasional private meetings with my advisor and committee members was advantageous for a few reasons. First, when my research was going in a positive direction, talking about my progress one-on-one with my advisor was helpful. In these meetings my advisor and I usually discussed new research ideas and future goals, an exchange that doesn't always happen in group meetings. This type of discussion helped ensure that my advisor and I were on the same page. Second, in a private meeting I was able to bring up other issues, such as conferences, setting dates for my preliminary exams and committee meetings, taking vacation time, and most important of all, working toward my graduation date. Professors often have a lot on their mind, and some of them have a dozen or more graduate students to worry about. So I believe it is important to keep committee members updated on your research progress. Third, setting up individual meetings also helped me build my relationships with my committee members. These meetings resulted in a more comfortable work environment and helped me build confidence in myself as a researcher. Finally, my committee members appreciated that I took the initiative to set up meetings with them. It showed them that I was thinking seriously about my future and my research.

In setting up meetings, I found that sending an e-mail seemed to work best. Professors spend a lot of their time (as you probably do too) answering and sending out e-mails, so the probability that they will answer your e-mail is pretty high. How soon they answer is another story. I have found that when a professor is taking a long time to respond, it is best to wait a week or two and then send a reminder e-mail or just casually stop by his or her office. In these circumstances, I found that professors usually remembered I had e-mailed them earlier and generally I received good responses.

When you do have a meeting scheduled with a committee member or your advisor, be prepared! Most professors have limited availability and I have found that my committee members appreciated it when I arrived at meetings with a list of topics to discuss. You want to make sure you are ready to discuss your work completely but also concisely so you have time to cover everything, especially if you are meeting with a committee member you haven't seen or talked to in a while.

Communicating research goals and a graduation timeline with committee members can be invaluable. By maintaining regular communication, I have enjoyed a supportive work environment and developed good relationships with my committee members. In addition, creating research and study plans in collaboration with the committee members has allowed them to serve as allies in reaching my goals and not just as evaluators of my work. Conversely, not sharing your plans can result in missed opportunities. My experience has been that committee members have a wealth of knowledge and good connections that can sometimes help you progress in a shorter amount of time than expected.

There will be times when your research goes very well and you get new and exciting data. But there will also be times when things do not work exactly as you planned. During my third year, I was having difficulty with the assembly of one of the peptide biomaterials I was working with. This was a material that was designed in my laboratory for cell culture and tissue engineering purposes. After numerous failed experiments, I decided to contact my biomedical engineering professor with whom I was collaborating. I knew as a graduate student it was important that I take the initiative and be responsible for my own research, so I decided to schedule a couple of meetings with my professor to discuss my experiment-related issues thoroughly and make certain that I was able solve them. After a couple of discussions, followed by trial and error, I was able to get the project back on track again. This experience helped me realize the importance of discussing my project with my closest mentors and fellow students; doing so really helped me move forward with my work. Once the experiments were working again, I got a manuscript ready and had it published several months afterward. Indeed, I was fortunate to have had the support of my biomedical engineering professor.

Two years later when I was applying for a postdoctoral position, the same professor was a member of my graduate committee and provided me with an excellent letter of recommendation. Because I had published with her, but even more importantly, because we had communicated so effectively with one another, she was able to write a detailed letter of recommendation that helped me get the position I wanted.

In addition to voluntary meetings you might schedule with committee members, sometimes departments require an annual meeting with a presentation to demonstrate progress. These kinds of reviews serve as a check to help guide graduate students. In my case, I found it really important to take advantage of these annual meetings to reinforce my relationships with my committee members and maintain their good impression of me. Here are three tips that helped me in those meetings.

1. First and foremost, I prepared in advance. Drafting this type of report usually takes a lot of time, and I have found it imperative to remember that the unexpected can happen. The flu or the blank blue screen of death on a crashed computer are impossible to predict. To guard against being thrown off by these setbacks, I started early, backed up my files regularly, and took the time to make sure I organized my data and wrote everything down as concisely and clearly as possible.
2. In the presentation I included a review of the goals of my project, along with the recent relevant literature. It also helped me to remember that it's okay if some of my data collection efforts were not successful. Despite best efforts, some experiments just don't work. Instead I focused on showing that I was knowledgeable about my project and interested and motivated to continue my work.
3. Listening and taking advice from my peers benefited me throughout my graduate studies. I practiced giving presentations in front of knowledgeable

colleagues and friends. Doing this also meant that I had to be open to criticism and new ideas. Hearing someone else's point of view helped me broaden my perspective on even my primary areas of expertise.

If by any chance you don't meet with your committee members outside of these yearly review meetings, do not shy away from contacting them by e-mail or just saying hello to them when you see them walking the hallways. Also, if you need advice about your project or your graduate career, don't hesitate to talk to them, as they can lend an ear and offer support. The more they get to know you, the better they can assist you during your graduate program and in your future career.

CONCLUSION

Like any other relationship in your life, the ones between you and your committee members require work. It has been my experience that taking the initiative early on to communicate and meet regularly with my advisor and committee members resulted in important and rewarding relationships. Meeting privately with your advisor truly does help you focus on your research, and expressing your ideas and goals in your meetings can help avoid confusion. It's a good practice to choose your committee members by seeking advice from fellow graduate students and then to maintain regular interactions. A close relationship with your committee can often enhance your research and dissertation, and lead to a solid job after graduation. I believe that by taking these steps you will discover that building a good relationship with your advisor and your committee increases your confidence and ultimately allows you to take control of your graduate career.

CHAPTER 5 GROUP DISCUSSION

As Charles explained, building a successful thesis committee involves making well-informed choices in selecting your committee members and then maintaining ongoing communication with them throughout the thesis writing process. His story offers good examples of healthy interactions with a thesis committee. As one might expect, however, problems in communicating with advisors and committee members can and do arise. When this happens, graduate students can sometimes face troubling issues that affect progress toward degree completion. How one prepares to avoid these potential pitfalls is a topic well suited for group discussion.

In the video created for this chapter, titled *Dilemma*, Isabella is ready to defend her thesis proposal before her committee, but encounters an unanticipated problem that disrupts her plan. Although the scenario depicted in the video is a little unusual, the stress and confusion that follow are not uncommon. The key is to recognize conflicts early before they become problematic and work to resolve such situations as soon as they arise. Following the video is a discussion activity in which a role-play exercise is presented that will give you a chance to think about solutions to Isabella's dilemma. The video and accompanying materials for leading a group discussion on this chapter can be downloaded from the chapter 5 resource web page at http://dx.doi.org/10.5703/1288284315203.

CHAPTER AUTHOR PROFILE

Charles M. Rubert Pérez, PhD

Dr. Rubert Pérez was born and raised on the island of Puerto Rico. He obtained his bachelor's degree in chemistry from the University of Puerto Rico–Mayagüez, where he carried out undergraduate research in the areas of analytical and organic chemistry. Dr. Rubert Pérez was also part of the Minority Access to Research Careers (MARC) and the Sloan Undergraduate Research Program (SURP), where he was introduced to graduate education in the sciences. After completing his bachelor's degree, he earned his MS and PhD degrees in chemistry at Purdue University. Dr. Rubert Pérez is currently at Northwestern University in Chicago working as a postdoctoral researcher in the area of biomaterials and tissue regeneration.

Chapter 6

Balancing Graduate School and Family

Joseph Chaney
Andrew Fiss, PhD
Francisco Iacobelli, PhD
Paul E. Carey Jr.

INTRODUCTION

Doctoral students commonly begin their graduate programs expecting to study harder than they did during their college years yet still hope to have a social life similar to the one they had before starting graduate school. Students who have a partner or a family are no different. While they may be expecting to make some financial adjustments and sacrifices in graduate school, in our experience, very few of them are ready for the many other ways their relationships with their partner and children, as well as extended family members and close friends, will be tested.

This chapter discusses these tests, their consequences, and how to deal with them. The authors recall some of their experiences with setting priorities, managing their time, preventing the stresses of school from spilling over into their family life, keeping in touch with family members when separated, and entering new relationships in graduate school. In offering these experiences, the authors explore some of the potential pitfalls as well as the strategies that have helped them to deal with their difficulties.

THE BALANCING ACT

Married with Children

While a part-time student trying to get a master's in computer science, Francisco realized that he wanted to work in academia. The prospect of teaching college students and being at the forefront of research was very appealing to him. Following his instincts, he applied to graduate school in the Chicago area, where he had built strong friendships and a rich social life over the previous seven years. He was engaged to be married and his fiancée was very supportive of his pursuit of his dreams. He thought that the next four years were going to be tough financially but eventually he would have his dream job. Francisco ultimately discovered that the road to the PhD was not so straightforward and that plans can and will change.

Francisco: There are a few things I wished I had known before applying to graduate school: that my program would take six years instead of the four I had envisioned; that I would become a parent within a year; that PhD students can have more than one advisor; and that one of my advisors would be a faculty member who was, at best, difficult to work with. Because I didn't know these things, I had to learn the hard way how to prioritize and balance my family and my studies. What follows is an account of that learning process.

I applied to a PhD program in January and met the woman that would become my wife in February. Go figure. To make a long story short, I got married in my first year of the program. Fortunately my advisor, a well-known researcher, spoke favorably about balancing work and family. I remember when I told him I was getting married. He got very excited and said, "That's great! We should have a party for you guys this Friday. Forget about your research for one day. There will be time to catch up." However, there was so much to do that I couldn't catch up. "You are behind in your work," he told me the following Monday. I was puzzled and pointed out that he knew this would happen. He explained that I could have worked Sunday night to catch up. I was left speechless out of frustration.

On another occasion, when I told him I was having a child, he again became very excited. We met and he pointed out what good progress I had made and how I could go back and plan a calm weekend with my pregnant wife. I began to feel stressed already thinking of what this calm weekend would really cost me in terms of work. That very Friday, right before I was leaving for home, I received an e-mail detailing a host of menial tasks that needed to be done before Monday. My throat tightened up and I felt sick to my stomach. I was used to having to work on my weekends, but it was so much worse now that I had made all my weekend plans and both my wife and I were counting on this time together. It seemed that the more he told me he understood my situation, the more he asked me to do menial tasks to keep me busier than before. I realized that my advisor's words about a healthy balance between work and family did not match his actions. He was overly demanding and abusive with power, but I figured a little of this was to be expected. My advisor worked very hard, and he probably expected his students to work, at least, equally as hard. Balancing life and work for him had a different meaning since work was his life.

Throughout my second year, he continued his abuses of power by asking me to do menial tasks whenever it seemed I had made good progress and could slow down for a bit. On a Friday during my second year, I remember scrambling to finish several tasks I was working on. As the clock approached 4:00 p.m., I became more and more optimistic that I would complete everything that day and have the weekend to myself. It was then that my advisor came over to ask me about my progress. I proudly reported that everything would be complete that day by 6:00 p.m., to which he responded, "Excellent! I have some other tasks I was trying to assign to you, but I wasn't sure you would be done today. However, now that you're finishing up with your regular work you can take care of these things. I need this stuff done by Monday," he added as he handed me a stack of material filled with tasks that were not urgent at all but that still, in his mind, needed to be done over the weekend. On his way back to his office, he even gave one of my officemates the all-important task of going out to the parking lot to remove a parking decal from his car. He seemed to relish the master-servant relationship. I was not alone in this opinion; all of us, his students and staff, would frequently talk about this difficult aspect of his personality when we were together. We were our own support group of sorts.

The many late nights I spent working on, and stressing over, research and menial tasks at the beginning of my studies were taking more than a small toll on my marriage. Every now and then I would take a step back and devote a weekend to quality time with my wife, but my advisor would soon rein me in by assigning me one of these menial tasks or making ridiculous threats. One day he even threatened to block registration for his graduate students if we didn't organize his files! It seemed as though he only wanted to display his institutional power, but I had to follow along because in my mind that was the only way to realize my dream. My wife would surely understand.

The latter part of my second year of graduate school saw the birth of our first son. I simply took the time off that was legally mine to take. As a university employee, which at Northwestern includes all teaching and research assistants, I had a right to take paternity leave. Even my advisor said that was okay, but as soon as I came back I was met with an insane pile of work. I had watched my in-box grow while I was away, but I had thought that my advisor was well aware that I was not going to work during that time. Of course he gave me a hard time when I got back to work. It seems he enjoyed taking away his students' happiness. Coming back to work after having a baby is a gradual process. Both the baby and the mother need a lot of attention and help at this time. Also, with children come visits to the doctor, unexpected visits to the emergency room, and so forth. My wife had a pretty strict schedule at work and since I was the one with flexible hours, I usually volunteered to go to these appointments. On one very cold winter morning our son was running a fever and my wife needed to leave for work. I told her I'd work from home that day and would take our son to the doctor. I sent an e-mail to my advisor explaining why I could not work at the lab that day and that I would finish the portion of my work that required the lab equipment the next day because it was not urgent. With that, I left for the doctor. When I got home some two hours later (pediatricians are always running late) I had the dreaded e-mail in my in-box. My advisor told me that I still needed to finish my work that day and that I could leave nothing for the next day. I replied to his e-mail saying that my wife was at work and that I couldn't leave my son. Then, he replied coldly with another e-mail in which he told me that my work was my responsibility, and my child was not an excuse to neglect my job. I thought then if this was the case, maybe I was not cut out for a PhD after all. However, I was proud, and I knew I was cut out for a PhD, so I just tested my metal and went back to work late that night and worked in the lab until 2:00 a.m. I was exhausted and had to go home to an angry wife and a sick child, but the work got done.

As the second half of my third year progressed, I tried to prioritize my family and reach a work/life balance. I still thought the problem was that I had not figured this out for myself. I was so focused on my goal, getting a PhD, that I was quite blind to how the toxicity of my working environment was seeping into my family life and undermining my priorities, quickly making me focus more on my PhD and less on my family. My level of stress was on the rise. I started to become depressed at times, cranky and anxious at other times. It seemed that I couldn't enjoy a family moment because I felt guilty about not working. A typical day after my wife and I arrived home from work went like this: She would say, "Hi honey. How was your day?" And I would respond, "Fine, but I have a lot of work to do. Bye." And off I'd go to my computer to work. If I ate any dinner at all, it was in front of the computer. Similarly, I was unable to enjoy social events. Dinners, weekends out with friends, happy hours—it all tasted like guilt to me. I was unusually severe with my kids and colder with my wife and friends. This was not me, the optimistic, positive guy who had started graduate school three years ago. I had to stop this.

When I realized that the current Francisco was not really me, I began to open my mind to other explanations for what was going on. With a new, open mind I started to actually pay attention to the advice of my wife and friends at the university. They had been telling me for over a year that no matter how much my advisor tried to make me feel guilty, the problem was not my work but my advisor and that he had created an abnormal environment and I should try to change advisors. University policies made it hard to change advisors though. For one thing, the new advisor would need to have money to fund me and, after a cursory survey, none of my potential new advisors had any money. After that first disappointment I gave up and started to fall back into being continuously stressed about potential tasks that I could be working on to advance my studies or please my advisor. My family went back to being my first priority in name only.

Things changed dramatically toward the middle of my third year. One day, at an appointment with the pediatrician, the doctor said that she was concerned with something regarding my son and that it was best that we took him to the emergency room. My wife and I were very scared and ran to the ER. I had been mildly concerned with work that I needed to do, but family emergencies like this have a tendency to take over everything else.

After hearing that my son needed to go to the hospital, I did not think of work, not for a second. After a full day at the hospital, at around 8:00 p.m., our fears were confirmed. Our son was seriously ill and we had to stay there with him for a few more days. Fortunately our son recovered during this stay, but once we left the hospital—with a clear mind that can only be obtained in an emergency, a mind that does not feel guilty for not working, a mind that is intensely focused on what is really important—I made my most crucial decision. I was going to become serious about prioritizing my family. The weekends would be sacred. During the workweek I would work exclusively from 8:30 a.m. to 5:00 p.m., and then if there was more work to do, I would do it after my son went to bed and after I had spent some time with my wife. If I couldn't accomplish this, I would quit the program. In other words, I was going to be in control. I was going to go back to being the person who started this PhD: the Francisco that can work hard, but who prioritizes family.

Things appeared to get better despite my advisor's attempts to make me feel guilty about work. This time I was firm in my priorities, and fate had a new advisor in store for me. In September of my fourth year I talked to one professor with whom I had a good rapport and whose work I liked. He heard my story and said he would be happy to be my advisor. At first there were problems because he lacked funding. I was so desperate that I even offered to pay for the remainder of my studies with my own funds and, perhaps, ask for a loan. Fortunately, in about a month he found out how to fund me and then took me into his lab. I spent the best three years of my doctorate working with his lab group. Family was first priority for both of us. Work was fun, not a burden, for both of us, and research was a process that involved mature discussions and not menial tasks for the sake of making my life miserable. I discovered that there were good advisors as well as bad ones. This seems obvious, but while I was too goal oriented and blind to the uniqueness of my circumstances, it was easy for me to miss this fact.

I was able to prioritize my family and take action to change advisors only after becoming at peace with the consequences that could follow these decisions. I had entertained these thoughts for a long time, but never with such a strong conviction. It was okay not to finish my program if it meant that I would be able to make my family my first priority in practice as well as in theory. These convictions gave me the determination I needed to successfully switch advisors.

My wife and I had two more children in the following years and, although it took me a little longer than expected—six years instead of four—to finish my studies, I did finish. I had to give up the idea of being the best researcher in my field, with the best publications, and so forth. Instead I valued being the happiest person I could be in an environment that allowed me to maintain my family priorities and still achieve the PhD.

Many students will be tested by tough or passive-aggressive advisors, circumstances outside of their control, and the unexpected twists and turns of life. For Francisco, balancing family life meant letting go of his initial vision of his graduate student lifestyle for one that allowed him to be happy, and which also was more functional and likely to give him the support he needed to achieve his doctoral degree. These obstacles can be hard to overcome, but with the deep peace that comes from knowing that you have set the right priorities, coping with the demands of graduate school does become easier.

Financial difficulties are the least of the problems for a family in which one of the partners is in graduate school. Setting the right priorities is a much harder challenge, as Joseph relates in the next narrative. For him, achieving success in graduate school was all about time management, as he describes.

Time Management

Joseph: We all know the old adage "time is money," but when you are in graduate school and have a family, this saying takes on a whole new level of meaning. In graduate school, time is like money because time becomes the most precious resource you have and, when managed wisely, you can have enough to meet your needs. Another principle in terms of energy management, the law of conservation of mass, states that matter cannot be created or destroyed. In graduate school, I learned that time is not similar to matter. It can be destroyed when it is lost. So now I say that time cannot be created or restored. Once it is spent, it is now in the past and cannot be recovered, so it matters what you do with it in the first place. I have had a lot of experience with both misspent and well-used time; however, time has never meant more to me than it does now as a graduate student with a wife and two young boys.

During the first semester of my first year of graduate school, students were expected to meet with different professors in the department to learn about the professors' research. During one of those meetings the professor and I began also to talk about my future goals in the program. I explained that I wanted to be an extremely successful graduate student and asked, "What commonality have you seen in your most successful graduate students?" Her answer was no surprise: the students with the best time management practices proved to be the better students.

The importance of time management in my life has been magnified ten times as a student with a family. When I first started school, I had a big ego and expected that I'd be able to do anything and everything with no problem. I thought I could handle the class load, pass all my qualifying exams on the first try, and cure cancer during my research time. These expectations would be demanding under normal circumstances, but then I became a new father. My wife and I discovered that she was pregnant while I was in the process of applying to graduate school. My son was born in June and I started school in August. I was not truly prepared for all the changes that would occur in my life once I became a father and the adjustment was difficult. Early in my graduate career, it often felt like there were not enough hours in the day to do my job, read papers for research, study for classes and qualifying exams, spend meaningful time with my family, and get enough sleep to do it all again effectively the next day. At the end of my first year, I realized that I couldn't remember the last time I had come home and spent any meaningful time with my family. Walking into a darkened house, with a sleeping child and a dozing wife, knowing I would be leaving for the lab again in the morning without getting to spend any quality time with them, I knew something had to change.

I spent the following summer semester assisting a professor while also sitting in on his class. After a few weeks the professor asked to have a private conference with me because he recognized that I was struggling. What began as his helping me to master different concepts turned into a really helpful mentoring relationship. I explained to him that I was a new father and that I had been working in industry for four years and hadn't been in school during that time, which had caused me to get out of the school habit. As he got to know me, he recognized that my biggest issue was how I managed my time, or more accurately, that I didn't manage my time at all. He then challenged me to be a better time manager and gave me several strategies to achieve this.

He taught me that I needed to be proactive about how I spent my time. Having some kind of plan would get me further than not having a plan at all. My plan needed to accommodate my personality as it applied to my work and my family. One approach I found effective was to be very detailed in my time management, scheduling every hour of the day and strictly abiding by it. The benefit of this approach is that with it I have a more predictable daily schedule. My family also appreciates this because they know what to expect from me and can include me in their plans. One limitation is that this strategy does not allow much flexibility, so another approach I have used involves a more generalist mentality. I schedule my research and family in blocks of time that are not as rigid but still planned. This gives me the advantage of having room in my schedule for things that may come up unexpectedly. A disadvantage of this approach is that because these schedules are not fixed, they can invite procrastination.

I have learned to apply these different strategies fluidly, based on the way things in my life are progressing at the moment. When I need to be a taskmaster to get things done in an efficient manner or to meet some deadline, I follow the first strategy. However, when things seem to settle down and all of my deadlines are weeks ahead of me, I tend to take the more general approach of taking care of things in blocks based on priority. This helps me to be the master of my life without being too stressed. My family is included in my scheduling process. This is important because they have needs that I have to consider and fulfill. They need my time. Frankly speaking, I had to make a decision that I wanted to be successful in both areas of my life: my academic life and my family life. Once I made this decision I was mentally ready to tackle this balancing act.

Learning how to effectively schedule my time has been very good for me because my life has only gotten busier as I've advanced in my graduate career. My wife and I have celebrated the birth of our second child, and the difficulties of research have demanded even more of my time. Looking back, when I had that first-semester meeting with my future professor, I shouldn't have just asked *how* to be a successful graduate student—I should have also asked what it *means* to be a successful graduate student. I now know that, for me, being a successful graduate student means using my time wisely to grow into the professional I want to be. My success is not determined by receiving the awards and accolades that I had hoped for when I started the program, but instead by meeting my program's requirements, publishing quality research, and completing my degree without sacrificing my responsibilities as a good husband and father.

Joseph's scheduling helped him to be a better student and a better "family man." You might find that you need to plan your days in graduate school much more than you did previously. Your professors, your advisor, and your colleagues might be able to offer advice about how best to do so. You also might discover that you need to change your professional goals to fit with your personal life. Periodically thinking about why you went to graduate school in the first place can help you regroup and reassess.

Networking, Family, and Friends

Graduate school has clear professional benefits, and yet it is not purely reducible to the end goal of a degree or a job. Focusing too exclusively on the end product means, to use a cliché, you ignore the journey. As Andrew learned in his first year, it is lonely and frustrating to be so goal directed. He came to realize that graduate school could be socially rewarding too.

Andrew: I have to admit that I probably should have given more thought to my decision to attend graduate school in the first place. I wanted a graduate degree because I thought it would validate all of the work that I had done through years of schooling, from kindergarten on. When I was a child, adolescent, and then college student, I was consistently rewarded for my diligence and wanted to push those study skills as far as I possibly could. Twenty-one years old and fresh out of college, I stepped onto Indiana University's campus, hoping for the same praise that I had received as a kid. I did not know how different graduate school would be from my previous educational experiences, and I had no idea that my expectations were unreasonable. Unfortunately, I think a lot of people approach graduate school in the same way.

A week after my first classes at IU, I e-mailed my girlfriend, who had just started a graduate program in England. "How was your trip?" I began. "How are your flat-mates? Have you discovered anything interesting about your program?" I then proceeded to describe in minute detail my assigned readings, my professors, and my grad student cohort. Much of her response was similarly factual and somewhat impersonal, but she ended her e-mail with, "I miss you a lot. I mean, frankly, I haven't had much time to miss you because I've been running around so much, but I've squeezed it into the nooks and crannies of my time."

Much of our relationship that fall was in sporadic free moments, the "nooks and crannies" of free time amid all our work, and over the course of a few months the time we spent talking became less and less. By November, we were sending one-line e-mails back and forth, which basically said, "I'm online. Where are you?"

Meanwhile, I stopped having time to call my parents. In September, we talked daily. In October, I called them every Sunday. But by November they started leaving messages on my voicemail: "Hi! We're just calling to see how you're doing. Give us a call back." And eventually, "We're worried something's happened to you. Let us know that you're okay," my younger sister, in the background, yelling, "I don't know why you have this cell phone if you never use it!" I listened to their messages over and over while walking back to my apartment at 10:00 p.m. Every night. I knew that they worried, but even then I was more concerned with getting all of my work done.

That fall was an absolutely miserable time in my life. I lived alone. I worked alone. I ate alone. It seemed I was always alone. I found myself having morbid thoughts. If something did happen to me, who would know? My girlfriend was in another country. My family was so far away that they might as well have been in another country too. I left for work so early and came back so late that I never had a chance to meet my neighbors. How long would it be before another graduate student or a professor noticed that I wasn't coming to any of my classes? Eventually, I started questioning my decision to come to graduate school. Why was I here in Bloomington? After all, I had been accepted to the university in my hometown. Why wasn't I there instead? I would spend hours fantasizing about what my life would be like if I had only pursued mathematics instead of the history of science, which required that I leave home for Indiana, or what I would be doing if I had taken that job with a large pharmaceutical company. I had lost the part of myself that loved being a student.

By February, I decided to make a change. I knew I needed to surround myself with people, so I became just as proactive about my personal life as I was with my professional life. I scheduled frequent get-togethers with friends: regular communal dinners in the middle of the week, lunches with classmates, and occasional trips to the movies on the weekends. I made sure to block out chunks of time for weekly phone conversations with my family and friends. Lastly, I decided that what I desperately needed was a roommate.

I awkwardly approached another student in my department about it. I thought he might laugh it off if I asked him bluntly, so I brought it up when we were passing each other on our way to class: "So, what are you thinking about for housing next year?" He thought for a moment: "I don't know." And I thought that was the end of the conversation. But the next day he e-mailed: "I was wondering what your housing situation is shaping up to be. Would you be interested in being roommates?" I guess he was feeling isolated, too.

My hunch about needing a roommate was correct. I learned that when I felt less isolated I gradually became happier, and I realized that I was very much mistaken about the point of attending graduate school. I had seen it as a climactic end to years of studies, but after I started prioritizing my personal as well as my professional life, I came to understand that I needed to see graduate school as a *lifestyle* instead. I had to find a way of making graduate school mentally sustainable. I needed to find a way to have a life outside of the classroom.

Today I am nearing the end of my graduate school career. In two months I will defend my dissertation. Three months after that, I will start work in a postdoctoral position at the college I attended as an undergrad. I am at the end of one journey and the beginning of another.

I did not stick to the strict timetable I set for myself when I was a first-year graduate student. I had many doubts along the way. I liked to fantasize about going into a variety of different careers, divorced from my graduate studies. These hurdles undoubtedly slowed my progress by a small amount, but mainly I had to slow down to enjoy my life at IU. I took extra classes in topics that interested me but that only tangentially related to my research. I designed and taught an original class that I passionately believed filled a hole in the university's course offerings. I joined a community choir. I became involved in student government. I visited my parents as often as I could. I attended my cousin's wedding. I went to a family reunion. Finally, my girlfriend and I got married. All of these things (my marriage especially) made me and continue to make me immensely happy. They were all worthwhile even though their combined effect meant I took one year longer to finish my program than I had initially hoped. That extra year has contributed more to my mental health than I can say.

As Andrew realized, it is often necessary to be proactive in your personal life, as well as your professional life, especially in graduate school. If you are feeling lonely or depressed, make sure to reach out to a friend, colleague, or mentor, but especially to your family and loved ones. Your mental health is more important than your academic success.

Building a Graduate School Family

Becoming comfortable in your graduate experience can be challenging, especially early on. Andrew became comfortable after reaching out to family and friends back home as well as making friends at school. Oftentimes though, it can be hard to keep up with friends and family back home due to location or timing, and some people are not very good at making friends on their own. Another way of getting comfortable in the new environment to which your graduate studies may have brought you is by tapping into graduate networks that already exist on your campus and building a graduate school family of sorts.

Paul became comfortable by building a strong support group out of the people he met in the campus groups he joined. This gave him a sense of family and provided a social group that he could go to events with, share ideas with, and just relax with when needed.

Paul: Getting into graduate school started out as an interesting venture. After sending out applications to a few universities and not receiving any replies, I started to question whether my hopes of going to graduate school would be realized. Luckily a simple clerical error was the cause behind my not receiving any responses and I was offered a contract within a week, once this glitch in the system was corrected. Although this was good news, I felt like I was now behind since I had been accepted late and did not get to attend the recruiting weekend, meet any of the faculty, nor interact with my fellow incoming graduate students. Missing all of these events really made me feel disconnected and uncertain about how my graduate experience had begun and how it would turn out.

When I arrived on campus for the first day of my first semester, I remember thinking, "What am I getting myself into?" And questioning if I was even fit to be there. I walked into my first class and felt immediately like I was the odd man out. Everyone was interacting with people they had already met, and I was basically there by myself. I had never really been the type of guy to force relationships to happen and I did not want to try to squeak my way into someone else's already formed group. After looking around, I also noticed that I was the only African American in the classroom. In fact, as it turned out, I was the only African American in my incoming class and, without having any relationships built yet, I felt I would be critiqued on every move I made. This really made me feel like I was an outsider.

That day, I decided I would prove I belonged. I came up with a plan where I would study all the time, go over my notes right after class was over, and make sure to have all my pre-class reading done before every class. Initially I was able to accomplish my plan of action, but I did not get the results I had anticipated. In many of my classes, fellow classmates had formed study groups, many of which seemed to have initiated from those early interactions in which I had not taken part. Because I'm a bit of a loner anyway, this did not bother me at first. I felt that I could do it all by myself anyway. But once we started getting some of our more challenging homework assignments back, I found myself looking at my low scores and feeling scared while around the room everyone else would seem to be smiling and joking. Their reactions made me feel like they had obviously done a good job on the homework assignments, which really made me feel inadequate. I think it was at that point I really noticed I was alone on my graduate school journey, and this feeling began to increase the amount of stress in my life. I am generally a calm and relaxed individual, but during this time I really allowed things around me to take a toll on me. On many days I would leave the lab, go straight home, and go to sleep. I found it hard to be motivated to study or participate in any activities. I was in a new situation where I had no one to communicate with or confide in. Although I was only an hour away from family, friends, and my girlfriend, they didn't seem to understand my situation, and I didn't have anyone to associate with at my university.

One day while walking down the hall of the chemistry building, I was approached by a fifth-year graduate student about a chemistry organization for minority students. I was familiar with this organization because it also existed at my undergraduate institution. She explained to me how the chapter here was in the start-up phase and that she would love for me to be involved in its development. At this time I was still feeling inadequate as a student and was unsure of adding anything else to my plate. Not only that, I was still so trapped in my introverted shell that I was scared to open myself up to anyone. I didn't feel comfortable talking about myself or my experiences in general. I could tell that she really wanted me to get involved though. She approached me many times about the organization and after multiple interactions with people associated with this organization, both professors and students, I decided to give it a chance and check it out. At the worst, I would have the chance to meet other individuals who seemed to have similar interests and goals.

I am so glad I did. I can still clearly remember those first few meetings, when we were having casual discussions pertaining to developing the chapter. Though I was initially quiet and kept to myself, there came a point where I was asked what I thought would help build the organization. I remember I really wanted to stay in my shell and remain guarded, but I thought, "What do I have to lose?" The worst I can do is to suggest a bad idea and never be asked another question again. I thought back to my undergraduate years, when I spent time in various organizations and I suggested many ideas. A few had even received positive reactions from the group.

For me this was a key turning point. Not only was I in an organization that catered to individuals with ideas similar to mine, but I was a contributor to the organization and people were listening to me and placing importance on what I had to say. During this time I really started to open up. I continued to be involved in this organization and started to notice that my physical and mental stress levels decreased. When I told the group about my classroom experience and my feeling that I was the only one struggling, they let me know that everyone was struggling. Just because I had not seen it on my classmates' faces did not mean that they weren't also having trouble with the course material. These simple words brought me tons of comfort. Even though I continued to struggle with my classes after this, I was more at peace knowing I was much closer to the pack than I had realized. To think, if I never had allowed myself to open up and become involved with this organization, I might not be on the path I am today.

Making friends in this organization gave me opportunities to talk with others about graduate school, life and its various struggles, and ways to overcome those struggles, opportunities that I did not previously have. Thanks to these individuals I gained more than just friends—I gained something of a graduate school family. I had formed a network that allowed me to feel at home in a comfortable atmosphere where I could be myself and feel a sense of relaxation. I realized how important it was to get out, get involved, and build a local support network at my university.

From that point forward I not only continued to be involved in that campus organization, but I also became involved in other organizations as well. During my time in these organizations, I occupied many positions from general member all the way up to president. I have been to national conferences, networking gatherings, and social events all because I allowed myself to step away from academics periodically and build meaningful relationships. I am so grateful for those who reached out to me, and now I make it my duty to reach out to others, especially those whom I see in a situation similar to the one I was in during my first year. I believe that in addition to all my experiences, I have become a more well-rounded person and a pretty good leader, which I expect will pay big dividends down the line, especially given the opportunities I now have to further my career through the network that I built.

Paul echoes the necessity that his coauthors emphasize for building strong relationships while in graduate school. If you are planning to attend graduate school without a partner or children, you might find it especially isolating. But, it is possible to build a network of friends by becoming involved in local and national organizations, especially in leadership roles. There is more to graduate school than academic work.

CONCLUSION

This chapter explored strategies that have helped these graduate students to strike a balance between their professional and personal lives. Francisco related how his decision to prioritize his family meant letting go of his initial ideal of graduate school. Joseph found that he needed to use a schedule to juggle all of his commitments. Andrew discovered that he needed to actively reach out to family and friends, not just to professional contacts. And Paul showed how it's possible to build a family out of grad school friends. All of their stories show how the division between the professional and the personal isn't as stark as they initially imagined. As they proceeded in their doctoral programs, they came to realize how all parts of their lives were interconnected.

Because individual circumstances are unique, the strategies shared will not work all the time. However, the stories shared illustrate some fundamental challenges for students attempting to balance their personal life with the amount of work required to obtain a doctoral degree—how to manage time with advisors, family, colleagues, and friends. You are encouraged to think about how you might have responded to their situations, and what you might have done differently. In addition, by understanding the authors' challenges, you may start thinking about how to deal with situations that may arise for you should you pursue a doctoral degree. Francisco, Joseph, Andrew, and Paul managed to come through successfully. So can you.

CHAPTER 6 GROUP DISCUSSION

The scenarios described in this chapter exemplify the need for proactive thinking and the ability to make changes so everyone's needs are met harmoniously. Not doing so can lead to some distress and complications in professional and personal life. This chapter is particularly well suited for a group discussion because of the great interpersonal variations that exist among people, families, colleagues, mentors, and friends.

In the video for this chapter, titled *Late Night,* you will enter into the after-hours life of Neil as he struggles to balance his academic and family life. The video and accompanying materials for leading a group discussion on this chapter can be downloaded from the chapter 6 resource web page at http://dx.doi.org/10.5703/1288284315204.

CHAPTER AUTHOR PROFILES

Joseph Chaney

Mr. Chaney is a graduate student at Purdue University starting his fifth year in biochemistry. He is married to the love of his life and has two beautiful children. Mr. Chaney worked in industry for four years before going back to school for his PhD with the support of his boss/mentor. He had been considering going back to school since he had started his career in industry, and it had always been his dream to be a research scientist. The catalyst that got the ball rolling was his experience with Hurricane Katrina, which taught him how precious the time we have in this life is, and that it is not good to put off one's hopes and dreams to a later date when tomorrow is not promised.

Andrew Fiss, PhD

While a senior at Vassar College, Dr. Fiss applied to a wide variety of graduate programs in pure mathematics, applied mathematics, and history of science. After many conversations with his academic mentors, he decided to pursue an MA/PhD in history and philosophy of science at a university hundreds of miles away from his friends and relatives. This made his transition to graduate school difficult, because in addition to feeling geographically isolated, he was also unfamiliar with some of the material that formed the core of his graduate training. However, he slowly became more comfortable in both his studies and in the broader university community. Dr. Fiss defended his dissertation in 2011 and subsequently has held postdoctoral positions at Vassar College and Davidson College.

Francisco Iacobelli, PhD

Dr. Iacobelli earned his PhD in computer science from Northwestern University. He got married right before he started graduate school and had three children during his PhD program. Dr. Iacobelli graduated from college in Chile, South America, and gained ten years of experience in consulting and computer systems both in Chile and the United States before going on to his graduate studies. He first earned a master's degree in computer science while still working. This changed his views on his vocation. Although he liked consulting, he found himself contemplating the possibility of entering academia full time and started his PhD program shortly thereafter. Dr. Iacobelli currently teaches in Chicago, where he lives with his wife and three children.

Paul E. Carey Jr.

Mr. Carey is in his last semester as a graduate student at Indiana University, majoring in physical chemistry. He is originally from Indianapolis and is involved in various organizations, including the National Organization for the Professional Advancement of Black Chemists and Chemical Engineers (NOBCChE), the Society for Advancement of Hispanics/Chicanos and Native Americans in Science (SACNAS), and the Alliance for Graduate Education and the Professoriate (AGEP), and he is a mentor for the IU-Groups STEM Initiative. He is also a board member for the Ian Smith Foundation, a nonprofit organization based in Indianapolis that focuses on giving back to inner city youth. Mr. Carey is married to a lovely young woman whom he has known since high school and enjoys participating in various intra-collegiate activities, such as intramural basketball, kickball, and football.

Chapter 7

Collaborative Research

Catherine F. Whittington, PhD
Kiana R. Johnson, PhD

INTRODUCTION

Collaborating with other researchers can be difficult, but it is also rewarding. Collaborative research presents challenges such as communicating effectively, negotiating different laboratory setups, and accommodating varied areas of expertise. These challenges become all the greater when collaborators are separated by large distances and work within multiple institutions. The payoff for dealing with these challenges, however, includes an expanded professional network, a broadened area of expertise, and new synergetic relationships that can create more possibilities for innovative research ideas.

In our experience with working with individuals in different areas from various institutions and departments, we have found that there are many types of collaborative research. In the majority of situations, each researcher has an expectation about the nature of the research relationship and the rights and responsibilities of each person. In this chapter, we describe some of the challenges and rewards we've observed in connection with collaborative work. More specifically, we discuss the importance of communication and data sharing, along with advance agreement on expectations such as authorship on publications.

HOW TO BEGIN COLLABORATIVE RESEARCH

As a graduate student, you will have many opportunities to meet researchers within your field. These opportunities can include conferences, workshops, seminars, and networking through your advisor. From our experience, research conferences and conventions have been the most rewarding in terms of meeting prospective collaborators. For example, each year Kiana attends the American Educational Research Association annual meeting. During this conference Kiana asks her advisor to introduce her to specific individuals with similar research interests. She also attends meetings for the division of the conference related to her field. This approach has been the starting point of communication for Kiana's collaborative projects.

Investigators often maintain relationships with one another based on successful past collaborations. Other collaborations may arise from a co-advising situation in which two faculty members are responsible for advising one student. In these cases, it is usually the professors who initiate the collaborative research project, which will then already be established prior to the graduate student's arrival. If you, as a student, join a collaborative project already in progress, it helps if you are able to integrate yourself into the project smoothly. The following story describes Catherine's experience joining a collaborative project already in progress.

←——→

Catherine: I spent my first semester of graduate school doing laboratory rotations within my department and I finally settled on a permanent lab at the beginning of my second semester. At the time, I was simply happy to have finally found my place in the department. I had no idea that I was also eventually going to be placed in the middle of a collaboration that would become my entire thesis project, from which I would learn a great deal about how collaboration works.

At first my advisor, Dr. Jones, assigned me to a project with one of the research scientists in the lab. The work was somewhat interesting, but honestly, I couldn't see myself focusing on that project for the next four to five years. I was more interested in a side project that one of the senior lab members, Adam, was working on as part of his thesis. The project was focused on wound healing, and I loved the idea that the research could lead to a product that could end up inside patients' bodies one day. As Adam would soon be graduating, his position on this project would soon be vacant. I talked with Dr. Jones about my interest in the project and asked if I could take over the project after Adam graduated. She agreed but said we would need to discuss this with the co-principal investigator on the project, Dr. O'Neal. At this point, I knew only about the research itself and was just vaguely aware that the project was part of a collaboration between two labs. Looking back on it now, I probably thought that the collaborator was more of a consultant. I definitely didn't realize how integrated Dr. O'Neal was in the project, or that he was in Indianapolis.

I knew that another student, John, worked with Adam on the project and that Dr. O'Neal was his advisor, but John was always around our department. He lived near campus in West Lafayette, took classes at Purdue, and worked in our lab quite often, so I wasn't sure why his advisor was located an hour away in Indianapolis. (For those readers who don't know, Purdue is in West Lafayette, Indiana.) I eventually learned that although John worked in our lab, he frequently worked in Indianapolis as well. It turned out that Adam also periodically traveled to Indianapolis to work in Dr. O'Neal's lab. I wasn't aware of the extra travel and had not factored it into my initial decision to join the project. I also had not considered that I would have to sometimes work in another lab. I now had a new set of questions, the main one being, What have I gotten myself into?

I was unsure if I was ready to commit to this type of project. I thought about how it had taken me about six months to find an advisor and lab that I felt comfortable working in for the next four or five years. I had believed that I was finished with my major first-year woes. I knew the people in my lab, the lab dynamics, and my advisor's work style, and I wasn't sure that I wanted to have to figure out these details all over again in a new lab. I didn't even know if this co-principal investigator in Indianapolis was going to like me, let alone want me working on his project. I had gotten so caught up with the idea of the project and its potential that I didn't stop to think about anything else that might come with it. Should I have just stayed with the boring project that held little interest for me? I wondered. At least I wouldn't have to deal with all of this extra stress that I hadn't seen coming, because honestly, I had never considered what this type of collaboration would require of me.

I had thought that collaboration was mostly just a label. You had someone to work with, but you only contacted that person periodically with questions or to share results. I quickly found out that the collaboration I was joining was going to be more than just data sharing. It was going to be an entire relationship, and I was going to be the new person in the relationship as well as on the project. In a nutshell, I had a lot to learn. I realized that I had much to consider about my situation, and I had to be quick about it. If I wanted to get out of this project, I would need to do it sooner rather than later so that I could still return to the other lab project if necessary.

After meeting with my advisor and Dr. O'Neal, who connected with us by phone, I realized that I may have been a little melodramatic about some of my early concerns. The two labs already had a working system that I could easily integrate myself into. After all, Adam had been doing it with success for over a year. Ultimately, Dr. O'Neal was fine with my joining the project and said that he would look forward to meeting me in person at some point. I then realized, Oh yes, I still have not met him. I only knew what his voice sounded like. I wouldn't even have been able to pick him out of a crowd, which left me slightly unnerved, but I had other things to occupy my mind, like learning how this collaboration functioned and what my responsibilities on the project were.

I was definitely aware of the learning curve that existed on this project. Even though John and I were in the same year of the PhD program, he was an MD/PhD student and had been working in both of our labs for two summers prior to my arrival at Purdue. Basically, he knew a lot more than I did, because I was starting from scratch on this project in more ways than one, adjusting to both the work and the new collaborators. I hoped that John would be willing to help me get up to speed. If not, I figured I was in for what might be a long, painful journey. Dr. Jones eased some of my apprehension by explaining that each lab had specific roles in the collaboration and that John and I would split the work accordingly. Our lab at Purdue was more of an engineering lab, while Dr. O'Neal's lab was a biological research laboratory affiliated with the Indiana University School of Medicine (IUSOM) at Indiana University–Purdue University Indianapolis (IUPUI). The collaboration would allow us to blend the two types of research by utilizing each of our areas of expertise. I'll be honest, it was a bit of a relief to know that I wasn't going to have to know it all, and I wasn't going to have to become an expert biology graduate student overnight. Before Adam graduated, I began to transition into his role on the project by learning how to set up experiments and by interacting more with John. The process was a little intimidating. John was friendly and helpful, but I felt like too much information was being dumped on me all at once. At the same time, it was comforting to know that I wasn't completely alone on the project.

Though I had been on the project for a few weeks, because of scheduling and the fact that his lab was in Indianapolis I still hadn't met Dr. O'Neal in person. I wasn't too nervous about meeting him because everyone said he was an easygoing guy, but I still wanted to see for myself how well I'd get along with him. It was always in the back of my mind that my work was to be evaluated by someone I still had never met face-to-face, and I couldn't help but be a little apprehensive about that inevitable meeting. Like anyone in my situation I wanted to impress him, so until we could meet in person I worked with what I had available to me. There was little opportunity to establish a relationship through e-mail. We only used e-mail to exchange information and transfer data. During this time though, Dr. Jones also had me sit in on some of the regular conference calls so that I could learn more about the current state of the project. I didn't have any experience with conference calls, so I just went with the flow and tried to follow the others' leads, mostly just listening and observing. In hindsight, I probably should have spoken up more during those calls. I could have asked more questions or tried to contribute to the conversation, but I was still a bit timid. I didn't get to truly meet Dr. O'Neal until after Adam graduated, and I was the sole graduate student responsible for the Purdue side of the project. As I became a regular fixture in the biweekly phone calls, I felt more like I was part of the project. I knew that I was going to have to take on a more active role during the phone calls though. I had to talk. I was hesitant at first, because I didn't want to say the wrong thing or sound naïve. I wanted very much, however, to make sure that Dr. O'Neal could tell that I was interested in the project and that I was capable of contributing. It didn't help that while I tried to speak up during the phone calls, I was also worried about the proper phone etiquette. It can be hard to interject into the conversation when you can't read a person's body language or facial expressions. The last thing that I wanted to do was cut off

Dr. O'Neal mid-sentence. Over time, the meetings got easier as I got more comfortable with the project and the collaborators. I learned that I didn't have to have all of the answers and that it was okay to ask questions; oftentimes, my questions were welcomed.

I finally did meet Dr. O'Neal in person later that semester, when Dr. Jones and I traveled to Indianapolis for a meeting with the IUSOM/IUPUI laboratory personnel. I was more excited than nervous about meeting Dr. O'Neal, with whom I was building a rapport over the phone. What really had me concerned, though, was finding the right location because it was my first time on the IUPUI campus. It turns out that I was right to have been concerned. I left my apartment, directions in hand, with plenty of time to make it to the meeting. I found the campus easily enough, but parking was another matter. After searching unsuccessfully for a place to park, I eventually decided to use the valet parking at the Indiana Cancer Pavilion. I walked into the building and started to look for the room only to realize that my meeting was actually at the Cancer Research Center a few streets over. I realized that I was now going to be late. I felt like I had ruined my chance to make a good first impression without even meeting Dr. O'Neal, but this fear didn't change the fact that I still needed to find the right place as soon as possible. As I was running late, I called Dr. O'Neal's office, got the correct directions, and hurried to the right location. When I arrived at the right room, I'm sure that I looked frantic. Dr. O'Neal just laughed at my little mishap though, and we started the meeting. We had the chance to talk when it was over, and Dr. O'Neal and John showed me their lab space before I headed home. After that meeting, I think that I finally felt fully integrated into the project. I also felt that Dr. O'Neal and I now had more of a complete working relationship. At least we now knew what the other person looked like.

As Catherine's narrative indicates, building collaborative research relationships can involve a number of steps, regardless of whether you played a role in starting the partnership. Collaborative research is not trivial, and it brings with it a set of challenges that researchers do not always encounter in traditional research situations, where virtually all parts of the research are handled in one location. People will usually learn very quickly that a great deal of communication is needed across the board and that trust among collaborators is essential. Each contributor to a project is responsible for a particular portion of that project, and each will in turn expect that everyone in the group will put forth his or her best effort to reach the end research goal.

COMMUNICATION AND DELEGATION

As in any relationship, it is imperative that collaborators maintain a healthy level of communication with one another. If you do not communicate well, you might be setting yourself up for an unsuccessful collaboration. Conversely, as illustrated in Catherine's story, good communication can enhance efficiency.

Catherine: I cannot say this enough: communication is the key to any collaboration. I know that if we were not in constant communication with our cohorts in the IUSOM/IUPUI lab, our working relationships would have become dysfunctional rather quickly. For us, it helped that both principal investigators held proper communication in high regard. It was an underlying element that could have made or broken the collaboration. The major duties and responsibilities of the project had been delegated prior to my arrival, and I was a little concerned that I really didn't seem to have much say in how assignments were being divided after I was fully integrated into the work. I quickly learned, though, that the division of labor was reasonable and that there was room for flexibility.

Our first priority was to play to our individual lab strengths, but if necessary, we could divide the work so that one person would not be overloaded. For example, our collaboration involved both long- and short-term experiments that were performed on the bench top and in animal studies. Because of our differing areas of expertise and lab capabilities, I primarily focused on the long-term culture experiments on the bench top that we performed on the cellular material manufactured in the Purdue lab. John focused on the short-term work and animal studies. However, occasionally I had to step in and work on some of the short-term experiments and perform the data analysis so that John could focus on the corresponding animal studies. These weren't my usual tasks, but I had to understand that no one ever said the work was going to be a fifty-fifty split. I needed to be flexible.

Animal studies are not trivial, and the ones John was performing required a lot of his attention, care, and time, which took away from his other work. If we wanted to continue to make progress, I had to step in, even though some of the work was not exactly in my comfort zone. At the same time, it was important that we communicated the change in tasks so that John wouldn't repeat the same experiments and waste time. There were other times when responsibilities shifted, but we were able to avoid any unintentional duplication of work or wasted time and energy by making sure that we communicated on a regular basis.

As Catherine points out in her story, it is easy to think that the research group in your individual laboratory can do it all, but even if they can, it may not be in the best interest of your research goal. Collaborations are generally formed because each member and each lab has something to offer toward meeting the ultimate goal. Drawing on the individual strengths of each member and dividing the work appropriately can shorten the time to completion and improve the quality of scholarship. Catherine's experience is an example of productive communication.

Breakdowns in communication may be intentional or unintentional, but either way, they can have a profound effect on the success of the collaboration. Here Catherine provides an example of a time that she encountered a breakdown in communication with one of her collaborators.

Catherine: John and I worked together for close to three years on the same project and had always been able to communicate well with one another. E-mail was our primary mode of contact since, like most students who have advisors at IUPUI, he moved to Indianapolis in the second year of his PhD program. Usually we would respond to one another within twenty-four hours. We never set guidelines on how quickly we would respond, but it just happened that way. Sometimes we would call if something was urgent or required a lot of explanation, but e-mail was our go-to communication method. Everything worked great until John graduated with his PhD and continued on to medical school. Even though he was no longer a graduate student in the lab, he understood that some things still needed to be finished, and he assured us that he would continue to work with us to finalize experiments and manuscripts. He promised that he would still check in with us and that he would be available through e-mail, but after he started his third-year clinical rotations, John would essentially go missing in action for months at a time. This wasn't exactly his fault. Rotations are rigorous and the schedule isn't designed for students to continue working in research at the same time. Anything beyond your rotation obligations was to be handled on your own time, and I'm pretty sure that John spent any extra time either sleeping or proving to his family that he still existed (which included his infant son). So, though we weren't surprised that it was tough to get in touch with John, we didn't expect that he wouldn't respond to us at all, which eventually became the norm. All of a sudden, we were left not knowing much of what was happening in the IUSOM/IUPUI lab.

Since John expected that he would be in the lab more often than he actually was, we had not transitioned his responsibilities to others before he graduated. Basically, he was the only person who knew his portion of the project, and for each of us to make progress on our portions of the project, the other collaborators and I needed to know several things. I e-mailed and waited; e-mailed again and waited. We asked Dr. O'Neal about John in our regular meetings, but Dr. O'Neal didn't have much to report either. He was waiting on a response from John as well. I felt like things had come to a screeching halt. I could make progress on parts of my work, but I still needed John's information for the majority of what I was hoping to accomplish. What concentration did he use for that chemical? How long did he stain with that dye? What is the product number for that antibody? Did anyone ever image those plates? Does anyone actually know where those plates are? Without the answers to these questions, I was essentially stuck.

Finally, Dr. O'Neal caught John in the hall of the hospital one day. As he put it, he grabbed John, snatched up a napkin and a pen, and had him write down anything that he could think of to answer our questions. Some questions were answered, and some weren't. We all realized, though, that our approach needed to change. John eventually scheduled an in-person meeting with the co-principal investigators and me so we could go over everything at the same time. He apologized for the lapse in communication, telling us that sometimes he was busy, or he would forget to respond to our e-mails. Other times he would just miss e-mails completely. To remedy this problem, John told us to harass him when we needed an answer. He also told us to call and leave him a message if necessary. We were productive at that meeting and got back to a point where we could move forward, but I felt like we had lost a lot of time and now would have to play catch-up.

←——→

Catherine realized that the normal method of communication that had worked when she and John were both graduate students was not nearly as effective when John's status changed. John's lab mates and Dr. O'Neal also found that they had not planned well for John's departure from the laboratory. All things considered, the collaborators learned that they needed to be flexible with their methods and styles of communication to reflect the ways in which circumstances had changed. This point is illustrated as Catherine's story continues.

←——→

Catherine: It took me a little over an hour to drive to IUPUI from my lab at Purdue, so early on in my project my collaborators and I determined that although we could meet in person when necessary, we were not going to be able to get together on a regular basis. It didn't make sense economically, and the commute would take quite a bit of time out of the day. E-mail was an obvious choice for quick communication and the relay of information, because we all use it daily and it is a handy way to transfer data, thoughts, and opinions. However, e-mail is not a perfect form of communication. One of the more stressful situations in research can be when you need an answer right away from someone, and he or she takes too long to respond, as indicated by my story above. Other obligations can keep people from responding to e-mails promptly, or they may miss messages entirely. Also, in my situation, what might seem urgent to me may not seem so urgent to my collaborators. While this difference in perspective is understandable, waiting on responses can be frustrating nonetheless. There were also times when I needed to share data that required a complex explanation. I would try my best to be precise and cover everything in an e-mail, but oftentimes it would end up being too long and confusing. Conversely, relatively simple e-mails could unintentionally turn into long drawn-out conversations that I would not want to have by e-mail. I definitely preferred more direct methods of contact for interactions like that.

The different participants in the project tried to meet in person periodically, but as that requires more effort and planning, we usually just talked during biweekly conference calls. I honestly believed that these conference calls were the foundation of our collaboration because they forced us to set aside time every other week to focus the project. We were able to share and explain results, ask questions, troubleshoot any issues, and get immediate feedback. When we did have the occasional face-to-face meeting where one group would travel to the other campus, the dynamics of our interaction were noticeably better. The physical presence of everyone shifts things because we could read body language and facial expressions. I didn't have to wonder anymore if Dr. O'Neal was frowning or smiling as I shared results over the phone, because I could just look at him and see for myself. For obvious reasons, these meetings made me nervous at times, especially if the data to be shared were not what we were hoping for, but the instantaneous feedback was invaluable.

COMMUNICATION OPTIONS

The kinds of interactions Catherine describes are helpful and effective in their own ways, because they reinforce the relationships between the collaborating groups. Both in-person and electronic communication can foster relationships between collaborators and maintain the integrity and success of the project, but each has strengths and weaknesses.

E-mail

Collaborators often use e-mail to communicate with one another, regardless of whether the individuals sit at the next desk or live three states away. E-mail has become a primary form of communication in general for many people, but in research especially, e-mail can be a valuable tool for sharing data and documents, planning meetings, and receiving feedback. It is one of the most effective and quickest forms of communication. But beware, collaborators in a research group can easily become overwhelmed with the number of e-mails they receive each day.

Pay particular attention to what you say in your e-mails and how you say it, because much can be misinterpreted. We have found that information might be misunderstood or be unclear. Be careful with the "Reply All" option. Many times you will want to use it, because all recipients need to see your message. However, the previous message and/or included information may not be intended for everyone. Answer e-mails sooner rather than later, because it is easy for an e-mail to get lost in your in-box. If you are unable to provide a response at the time, make sure that you have a system for keeping track of unanswered e-mails. Suggestions for a system may include marking these e-mails as unread, tagging them with a priority designation, or moving them to a special folder.

Phone/Video Conference

We have discovered that although in-person meetings are important for maintaining communication between collaborators, they can be difficult to achieve if collaborators are located far from one another. The logistics of a conference call can be a little tricky, but the availability of many different forms of technology have made it so that most people are able to participate in conference calls, either by phone or video, with collaborators if meeting in person is not an option.

It is easy to fade into the background during a conference call, especially phone conferences. You might feel hesitant to interrupt or jump into the conversation, but if you have something to say, you will have to do it eventually. Wait for a pause in the conversation and do your best to make sure that the previous speaker has finished. If you speak up and that person continues talking, let him or her finish and then begin. Most likely, the previous speaker will defer to you anyway, because you spoke up. A video conference is a little easier in that a subtle signal such as a raised hand or a short wave can let someone know that you have something to say. Conference calls are not always the perfect form of communication, so be prepared for a few snags here and there. Sometimes connections are not optimal and may result in spotty reception. You might need to end the call and attempt to reconnect, or try a different avenue. A cell phone, although handy, may not be the best phone to use. If you are confident in the connection you might try it, but if a land line is available, it is usually the more reliable choice. Additionally, there could be difficulties in setting up the call because of a system incompatibility, so it is best to test the system beforehand.

In-Person Meetings

As Catherine indicated in the previous section, face-to-face meetings are arguably the best. Most of us are used to meeting with people in person, but here are a few things to think about when meeting with your collaborators.

Since these meetings may be few and far between, they need to be productive. Preparation is the key. If you and your colleagues have not outlined an agenda prior to the meeting, it is important to settle on an agenda at the start of the meeting. An agenda will help the meeting flow better and ensure that all points are covered. Furthermore, arrive at the meeting on time. If you have to travel to the meeting, allow extra time for delays, and always contact others in the group if you are going to be late. Also, if any additional tasks are to be undertaken at the meeting (e.g., supply transfer, laboratory work, demonstrations), everyone needs to be aware of the plan prior to the meeting. These types of meetings may be difficult to organize, but you should definitely make an effort to meet periodically with your collaborators in person, if possible.

File Sharing

Technology has allowed us to share information across institutions with relative ease. As mentioned previously, e-mail can be used to share data and documents. It is quick and easy and most people have access to it the majority of the time, but it does have its limitations. If a file is too large, certain e-mail clients may take too long to transmit it, or the recipient's client may not be able to accept the file. An alternative to e-mailing information is to upload it to a hosting site through your university or a third-party host. Once you provide your collaborators with the link to the file location and a password, they can access the file. Make sure that you are familiar with the rules and guidelines with these types of sites. If the site is restricted to temporary storage only, you will need to make sure that everyone is aware of the time frame for accessing the information.

AUTHORSHIP

After working together on a study or in the lab, collaborators often publish their findings as coauthors. This process inevitably raises the question of authorship. Determining who will be the first, second, or third author and so on, as well as who will be listed as a contributing author, is important in a research project, but it can also be uncomfortable. As a graduate student you may not even have a say on your position in the authorship order. For instance, if you are working on a project with one of your professors, as in Catherine's example earlier in this chapter, your professor might take the first author position. If you find yourself in a position where you do have a say on your position in the authorship order, it is usually best to be upfront about your expectations and to make sure you know your collaborators' expectations as well. Waiting until the end of the writing process to broach the topic of authorship order may create unease, or even open conflict, among the group's members.

Academic publishing is a professional activity, so it is reasonable to expect that people will behave professionally when negotiating authorship. If you are honest and polite in claiming the credit you believe you deserve, people will most likely respond in kind, even if they disagree with you, though of course there are always exceptions. Kiana learned the importance of establishing early the order of authorship for a collaborative article during her first opportunity to publish. She was fortunate to have had an advanced colleague working with her who guided her through the process of determining authorship order and collaborating with others as the first author, and as Kiana's story demonstrates, when that collaborative process changed, everyone working on the article knew in advance how that change would affect the authorship order.

Kiana: During the spring semester of my fourth year as a graduate student, I collaborated in writing an article for publication. A group of my colleagues agreed to write an article with me based on data from a study I had completed a year earlier. Needless to say, I was both excited and flattered that my colleagues had taken an interest in my research. The study investigated the relationship between parent/child communication and the child's achievement and adjustment in school, which is related to my main research area, albeit a bit tangentially. As this was to be my first publication, I was happy to revisit an old research interest and deviate a little from my primary research area for a short while.

Initially I was a bit intimidated, especially because my coauthors suggested I should take the first author position on the project. One of the colleagues with whom I was going to be writing the article was far more advanced in her career than I was in mine, and this fact made me feel unqualified to take the lead. However, after thinking it through, and with much encouragement and support from my collaborators, I decided to take the risk and agreed to be first author on the article. I was really invested in the project as we started the writing process, but as the collaboration progressed and time went on, my interest in the topic waned. I had enjoyed conducting the study the year before, but as I returned to the topic during the writing process, it became less and less exciting for me. Plus, I realized that I had underestimated how much the work on this article would interrupt my primary studies and research tasks. What I expected to be a small deviation for a short amount of time quickly became a very disruptive drain on my schedule. My more advanced colleague picked up one writing responsibility after another that was initially supposed to be mine.

Fortunately, before we had begun writing the article, my senior colleague had asked me to meet in order to discuss the article and my role as first author. I had gone to her office on campus that day feeling unsure about what was expected of me and intimidated about taking the first author role altogether, but because she had already written many articles, I figured I would get great advice. I was grateful that she intended to mentor me through this process. She was very informative and provided me with a few articles about publications and authorship that had been published by the American Psychological Association. She explained that as first author, I would do the bulk of the writing, and the rest of the coauthors would add their contributions to my mine. She also stipulated that because I was the first author and had completed the study on which the article was based, it was my responsibility to complete the method section. Finally, and as it turned out, most importantly, she pointed out that with research projects, sometimes the authorship order changes to reflect the reality of who completed the majority of the work on the article. Because of this conversation in which we had discussed all of the eventual outcomes of our collaboration, when I did step back and let my colleague take over my writing responsibilities, it wasn't awkward when we also decided to switch the order of our names as authors.

Although it turned out well, this situation had the potential to be a disaster. For instance, if I had let my coauthor takeover my writing responsibilities but later refused to give up the first author position, or if my coauthor took the first author position without first consulting me, feelings could have been hurt, collaborators could have become upset with one another, and the whole project could have ended without publishing the article. But because my colleague knew how important it was to set up expectations in advance, we avoided this outcome. It is easy to change from one order of authorship to another if the guidelines are predetermined and agreed upon by all collaborators. Because my collaborator and I discussed authorship before and during the writing process, neither of us resented the other when the authorship roles reversed. Although it may seem like this discussion would have been tense, it wasn't at all. All the collaborators knew the expectations and responsibilities of each author in the group and that this order could change at any given time, so when it happened, no one was taken by surprise.

CONCLUSION

When collaborators are direct and honest with one another about their expectations for the process once the project has commenced, the benefits can extend beyond the duration of the project. The professional relationships researchers develop in collaborative work can be very valuable to all involved. Researchers will often work with one another again and again based on the effectiveness of their initial collaboration. The synergistic productivity of collaboration is hard to match when working individually, but one must remember that this productivity is almost always contingent upon the researchers' communicating well with one another, being open and honest about their expectations, and being flexible in response to changes in the collaborative relationship. Fulfilling these criteria will not guarantee you a successful collaboration, but it will help you be a better collaborator, which is a large part of the challenge of collaborative work as a whole.

CHAPTER 7 GROUP DISCUSSION

Group collaboration in the research and publication process is at the heart of academic life, and the scenarios Catherine and Kiana have related in their stories give an informative introduction to this life of inter-collegial success. As with most interpersonal relationships, open and clear proactive communication in these collaborative relationships is the oil that keeps the synergistic process running. When each participant's involvement in the project has not been clearly defined from the beginning, complications can develop.

The video for this chapter, titled *Who's First?*, takes you into the world of collaboration, where Kaleah and Suzanne combine efforts on a project. The collaboration begins with great enthusiasm but ends in a dispute. In the group discussion activity, you will enter into a role-play where you become the arbiters of the dispute. During the discussion, you will deal with some of the hazards and some of the solutions to conflicts encountered in graduate student collaborative relationships. The video and accompanying materials for leading a group discussion on this chapter can be downloaded from the chapter 7 resource web page at http://dx.doi.org/10.5703/1288284315205.

CHAPTER AUTHOR PROFILES

Catherine F. Whittington, PhD

Dr. Whittington received her PhD in biomedical engineering from Purdue University in December 2012. Originally from Hallsville, Texas, she graduated with her BS degree in biomedical engineering from Louisiana Tech University. In addition to her activities with AGEP, she was also active in K-12 and undergraduate outreach with the Purdue Biomedical Engineering Graduate Student Association and the Purdue Black Graduate Student Association. Dr. Whittington is currently a postdoctoral scientist in oncology research at Eli Lilly and Company in Indianapolis, Indiana, as a part of the Lilly Innovation Fellowship Award program.

Kiana R. Johnson, PhD

Dr. Johnson recently earned her PhD in educational psychology at Purdue University, where she also earned her BS degree in psychology. She is from Indianapolis, Indiana, and attended public schools. Dr. Johnson enjoys her research, which focuses on youth with chronic health conditions, and also serves as an advocate for these youth. She is currently a postdoctoral fellow at the University of Minnesota with the Leadership Education in Neurodevelopmental Disabilities program. Her current research focuses on the transition from pediatric to adult healthcare for youth with physical disabilities.

Chapter 8

Graduate Student Support Programs

Cyndi Lynch
Kathy Garza Dixon, PhD

INTRODUCTION

The pursuit of a PhD is a rewarding journey that provides numerous opportunities to develop as a student, a scholar, and a citizen. These opportunities typically vary as graduate students progress through their programs, culminating in experiences that individualize the degree recipient. Completing a PhD represents a significant accomplishment, but achieving this goal may require learning new skills along the way. Therefore, most colleges and universities offer several support programs to help graduate students succeed.

In this chapter, we share stories from our experiences as student support program directors based on our students' experiences that highlight some of the opportunities and challenges that graduate students can encounter. Through these narratives, we discuss some typical programs and services designed to support doctoral students along the road to the PhD.

Simply put, our message to you is this: *seek out resources and reach out to others.*

DEVELOPING SUPPORTIVE PEER RELATIONSHIPS

For many students, graduate school is a new beginning, usually in an unfamiliar location with new and socially diverse groups of people. Consequently, as Cyndi relates, issues of adjustment involving the discrepancies between the imagined and the actual are a common concern for many of the graduate students with whom she meets. Some students try to make the adjustment to the graduate school environment on their own, while others seek support from outside sources. Teneka and Natae were two first-semester graduate students beginning a doctoral program in the same department at a campus in a town new to them. Cyndi relates the stories of their struggles with different issues of adjustment to the new world of graduate student life.

Cyndi: When Teneka first arrived in my office, I asked her how things had gone for her in her first week of graduate school. She began telling me about all the activities and meetings in which she had been involved, along with all the tasks she had completed since her arrival. As a first-year graduate student, she arrived on campus one week early, as directed by her program chair, to attend the weeklong orientation sessions. Monday morning began with the expectations of the graduate program followed by sessions on registering for courses, completing payroll procedures, enrolling in a medical insurance plan, and obtaining a student identification card. The remainder of the week was focused on completing university-mandated trainings in lab safety, academic integrity and plagiarism, responsible conduct of research, equal access and equal opportunity, and the Family Educational Rights and Privacy Act (FERPA) requirements. These trainings were necessary before Teneka could begin her teaching and research duties. She finished the week by attending the teaching assistant orientation, the Graduate School orientation, and the Graduate School Resource Fair. Her final on-campus task for the week required her to hike across campus and obtain her department's signature on the parking permit form, then walk back to the parking office and obtain the permit. The orientations seemed endless, and at the same time she had several tasks demanding her time and energy, such as settling into her office, buying her books, and organizing her apartment. Although Teneka had been determined to unpack a few boxes each evening, she was too tired from reviewing the orientation materials to unpack at night. In spite of her best intentions, she was still living out of boxes after the first week. She had yet to venture out to the local grocery store for food and household supplies.

As I listened to Teneka tell her story, I soon realized how task-oriented she was. She seemed to be well organized and generally pleased with her completion of all the orientation sessions, given the hectic agenda for the week. Despite her progress, however, she was worried about reviewing and understanding the orientation materials, unpacking, and prepping for the first week of classes. I was a little concerned that she had not mentioned any other students by name or discussed any new relationships, so I asked Teneka about new friends. That's when she told me about meeting Natae.

Teneka met Natae, a fellow first-year graduate student, during the orientation for teaching assistants. Natae had suggested that they attend the department social together. The social, organized by the Graduate Student Association, is a meet and greet with faculty members and graduate students in the department. Natae had said that the advanced graduate students would be available to answer questions that the first-year students might have, and that they could learn more about how the department works. Teneka declined to join; who had the luxury to attend departmental social events? Her to-do list was endless. She needed to unpack, organize her apartment, figure out the directions to the grocery and discount stores, and prepare to teach her first class on Monday.

As our meeting ended, I encouraged Teneka to establish relationships with her department colleagues as well as people outside of her department. These would be people to whom she could turn for social and academic support. She nodded in agreement and set up another appointment for later that week.

A few days later, Natae came in to see me. I asked how she was adjusting to her graduate program. In contrast to Teneka, Natae began her story discussing her new relationships. Natae was disappointed and hurt by Teneka's refusal to attend the department social with her. She was feeling alone, anxious, and overwhelmed in this new environment, facing many unknowns, including whom she could trust and what was expected of her. Could she meet the expectations required in her course work, in teaching, and in research? It would have been comforting to have another new student like Teneka at her side at the department social. With her network of peers, friends, and family geographically distanced from her, Natae's confidence in her abilities was waning. Her social network during her undergraduate years had always provided her moral support, motivated her, and helped her identify resources and support programs for her undergraduate success. Natae also had used her network to understand the expectations for graduation and to plan her career development. Natae attributed part of her success to this supportive network. Therefore, establishing her contacts with new peers and friends was an immediate goal she knew would support her success as a graduate student. Although Teneka had declined her invitation, Natae still attended the social, where she learned more about the department expectations and practices, identified colleagues for her mentoring network, and learned about mentoring resources housed in her home department and the Graduate School, such as the *e*Mentoring program. The *e*Mentoring program matched Natae with advanced graduate students who could serve as peer mentors to support her in successfully fulfilling her academic, teaching, and research responsibilities. For Natae, the department social was not a luxury, but an essential component in developing her social support system for success.

As we discussed her experiences, I realized how important relationships were to Natae and to her identifying and meeting the expectations of the graduate program. Natae admitted that she was confused and hurt by Teneka's response to her invitation and her decision not to go to the social. Not only did she feel the sting of rejection, but she was concerned that Teneka was missing valuable information to help her succeed in her graduate program. However, Natae vowed to reach out once more to Teneka.

When the time arrived for Teneka's next meeting, I was not surprised to see both students walk into my office. Natae's persistence in extending invitations had paid off. Teneka had joined the *e*Mentoring program. Natae and Teneka were meeting regularly to discuss departmental expectations, teaching issues, and other topics. They seemed to be off to a good start.

← →

As a graduate student mentor, it was rewarding for Cyndi to see that Teneka and Natae had come together and were able to support one another and avoid the social isolation commonly encountered when transitioning to the graduate school environment. In contrast to Cyndi's story, Kathy tells about a situation in which the student who came to see her had lessons to learn about just saying no and remaining focused on the key responsibilities graduate school requires.

LEARNING TO SAY NO

Time management and self-discipline in graduate school are two major areas that challenge graduate students. In my role as a program director, I work with students who often share frustrations and experiences that they are reluctant to share with their advisors, professors, and supervisors. The opportunities for involvement in college can seem limitless, and involvement in too many extracurricular activities can add undue stress. Fortunately, there are support programs throughout the campus that provide aid to students on a variety of topics. Often, you need to take the initiative to seek out help; other times the support can come from unexpected places, such as your peers.

The following story is about a student who found it difficult to say no to student activities, and the consequences that resulted.

Kathy: About four weeks into the fall semester, a student came into my office obviously upset. I asked her to sit down and I immediately closed my door so we could have privacy. The student, Shelley, started to cry and told me she wanted to quit school and go home. Of course, she wasn't the first student to come in and say this to me. I gave her my undivided attention as she started to tell her story.

Shelley's story began with the August day in San Marcos, Texas, when she and her parents set off on the long three-day drive up to central Indiana. Shelley's parents were especially proud of their daughter, who was pursuing her PhD in chemistry. She was not only the first in the family to be accepted into graduate school, she was also the first in the family to obtain any college degree. They had rented an apartment in West Lafayette for Shelley using an online apartment locator, so her parents were a little nervous about seeing the accommodations they had arranged. Her father and mother had high expectations for their very smart daughter. Shelley wanted more than anything to get her PhD and become a professor at a good college, so she could make her parents proud and hopefully help them financially. As the first person in her family to attend graduate school, she was apprehensive, feeling the weight of responsibility on her shoulders.

They were all thrilled that after the long trip, the apartment looked as good in real life as it had been presented in photos on the web page. They spent the weekend checking out the area, and on Sunday her parents got on a flight back to Texas. After they left, Shelley felt lost without her parents' company. Yet she knew that somehow she had to make it work and make her family proud.

Shelley continued her story starting with orientation week, which began bright and early on her first Monday morning at Purdue University. Shelley had a teaching assistantship in the chemistry department, so she had to go to all of the orientations for this job. She attended the general meeting with the other grad students and faculty, her teaching meetings, her lab group meeting, and a meeting with her advisor. In addition, she attended the various informational meetings aimed to prepare students for graduate school. Plus, there were endless call-outs and evening events for scores of student organizations on campus. Shelley didn't want to miss anything. She went to as many of the orientation week events as possible but got home exhausted every night.

In spite of the intense demand on her time and energy, Shelley kept up this very fast and frantic pace. She joined a cooking club so that she could maintain a healthy diet. She also joined a workout group that met three times a week and alternated workouts between aerobics, Pilates, and kickboxing at the student recreation facility. She joined the Graduate Student Council. This seemed like a good way to make meaningful connections on campus and it would give her the chance to network with responsible graduate students in other departments. Next, Shelley met with students who were members of a graduate minority club. Joining this club seemed like it would help her as a minority student on campus, and she would have a way of meeting other first-generation Hispanics going to graduate school. She couldn't believe all the great things there were to do and to get involved with at Purdue University. The clubs and activities were so much more appealing than those at her undergraduate college, and the benefits appeared to be limitless.

Shelley was exhausted at the end of orientation week. She had been out extra late on Friday night during the welcome social event, which was sponsored by the minority club, and had met some great people, including Bobby, who seemed like he could become a good friend.

Shelley slept very late on Saturday morning. Once she woke up, she anxiously remembered all the stuff she had to do for school on Monday. She was particularly nervous about teaching. This class would be the first time she had ever taught. It was an introduction to chemistry class. Then before she could head out to go to the bookstore, her cell phone rang. It was her mom and dad. Shelley answered right away to hear her mother's voice. "Shelley, where have you been all week? We have been trying to call you and you never answer your phone." Shelley managed to get her parents calmed down and to reassure them that everything was under control and that she would do her best to call them regularly from now on.

Shelley set out to buy her books for her graduate courses. It took forever to find parking, and the students swarmed the bookstore. Fortunately, she got all the books she needed except for two, which were both sold out. What a headache! She knew better than to wait until the last minute.

When she got home, she opened her e-mail to contact her chemistry listserv; she hoped someone would have the textbooks she needed. She was overwhelmed when she noticed her in-box was packed with mail from all the groups she had visited and whose e-mail distribution lists she had joined. She picked through all the e-mails and found an unexpected message from her advisor and lab director, Dr. Mullen. He had already assigned a reading from the textbook that was sold out. The next urgent message concerned a Graduate Student Government meeting. Not good timing—it was planned right before her Chemistry 101 class, which she had to teach. She was happy to see a message from Bobby, the guy she had met at the minority social; he wanted to get together and study this week. She found the syllabus for her Foundations of Chemistry seminar on Thursday morning and realized there would be a quiz at the end of the week. Shelley sighed as she said to me, "I knew then that this was going to be an interesting semester."

As she continued with her story, I began to understand her dilemma. Shelley desired a sense of community and hoped to gain this by becoming involved with as many activities as she could find on campus. Campus involvement can be a very positive factor in succeeding in school; however, as with everything else, moderation is the key to success.

On the evening prior to her first day of teaching, Shelley received an e-mail from Bobby stating he had materials that would help her create her lesson plan for her class. Unfortunately, he arrived after 10:00 p.m., which left her little time to prepare. She went on to describe her first day of teaching. It was a disaster! She was running late for class, and the students were rude and disrespectful. They were loud and did not quiet down when she was trying to lecture. She was a nervous wreck and felt she did a terrible job reviewing the syllabus and explaining her expectations for the semester. When she tried to describe some of the simplest concepts that she would cover, the students looked bored and inattentive. After class, she went to the women's restroom and cried. She felt like she had to be the worst teacher in the world! She was humiliated and just knew the students were laughing at her as they left. She said with a tone of real frustration, "It might have helped if I had been more prepared."

After teaching, she went to aerobics class and then met with the minority club planning committee. Shelley had volunteered to help plan activities for diversity awareness week, which was scheduled for mid-September. Late and frantic, Shelley rushed to make it to her first class, slipping into the back of the room while the professor was already lecturing. She was embarrassed but hoped the professor had not noticed her. Unfortunately it was Dr. Caleb's class. He was the professor who had given her the teaching assistantship. She knew she should stop by after class and talk to Dr. Caleb about her terrible teaching experience, but she could not bring herself to address it just yet. Regretfully, she was not in the right frame of mind to be an attentive student.

Shelley continued her story and told me about the great opportunity she had been offered by her advisor, Dr. Mullen, to work with him and two other graduate students on a research project. She knew that she was very fortunate to get this chance to start working on research during her first semester. She attended the meetings on Monday and Wednesday evenings and had already met individually with Dr. Mullen to discuss her part of the research. Last week everything caught up with her after spending a late night out at a local pub with Orlando, a new friend she had met at the gym. By this point, Shelley was extremely tired. She arrived late for the Monday evening meeting with her professor. She had a difficult time concentrating on the conversation. She tried very hard to focus, but her eyes felt very heavy. Her head kept dropping. Instinctively, she caught herself, reflexively jerking her head back into an upright position. It was embarrassing because she knew other members of the research group were noticing her, but she didn't think her professor had noticed. By the end of the two-hour meeting she was physically drained; she went home and collapsed on the couch, only to be awakened by the telephone. It was her father complaining about her not calling. She felt terrible—she had missed her mother's birthday!

In an attempt to make up for her forgetfulness, the next morning Shelley stopped by the flower shop on her way to school and ordered a huge bouquet of flowers to be sent to her mother. She hoped her mom would forgive her. However, the stop at the flower shop made Shelley late for her first graduate class. The professor embarrassed her when she walked in late, telling her, "In the future if you cannot be on time don't bother coming." She could feel the eyes of all her peers on her. The day continued on a downward spiral.

To make matters worse, her advisor, Dr. Mullen, called her into his office. He addressed her tardiness and inability to concentrate and informed her that she was in jeopardy of losing her position on the research team. Shelley felt so overwhelmed. The final straw was the fact she had received a failing score on a test that accounted for a third of her grade in her analytical chemistry course. She had failed her first test ever!

Shelley told me she had called her parents last night to tell them she was failing, and they immediately told her they would come and get her and take her back home. She would have loved to go home and be around friends and family again. But the thought of going back home without her degree was unbearable. Thinking about her parents again, she started packing her bags and was halfway packed when Bobby showed up with pizza wanting to study together.

I realized then it was her friend Bobby who had encouraged her to talk to me about leaving school. He had once been in a very similar situation and had come to discuss his issues with me. So I turned the discussion to possible ways Shelley might lower her stress, much of which included learning and incorporating time management techniques into her daily routine. We also discussed her being homesick and I gave her a few possible suggestions. I asked her to come back and see me if she wanted to continue the discussion.

Shelley returned to my office the following week and her spirits were higher. She told me things were looking better. She had completed the time management worksheet I gave her, realized that she had overbooked her time, and was in the process of eliminating things from her schedule. She dropped her workout group and opted to follow an individualized exercise plan that would easily fit her schedule. She explained her situation to members of the various groups she had joined and promised to stay involved, but to a lesser degree. She still had concerns about her teaching abilities and was embarrassed to talk with her advisor. We discussed these issues and she determined that an honest, candid discussion with her advisor was required. She also needed a similar discussion with her parents. They were very concerned and wanted her home.

Two weeks later Shelley and Bobby entered my office. Bobby seemed to be a good influence on Shelley. He had coached her on limiting her involvement with campus groups. Shelley had talked to Dr. Mullen and was given a second chance on the research team. She had been punctual for every meeting during the past two weeks. Bobby had suggested she talk to her other professors concerning raising her grades. She had been attending her professors' office hours and was feeling confident that she could raise her grades by the end of the semester. Also, Professor Caleb told her of resources in the department to help her with her teaching techniques and provided names of other graduate students she might want to meet with who were teaching the same course. The last hurdle was dealing with her parents.

Shelley knew that her parents really wanted her closer to home, but she was not ready to give up on her dreams. She decided to fly home on her first long weekend. Once home, she talked to her parents about adapting to graduate school and how she was starting to correct some of the behaviors that had led to her stress and anxiety. She openly discussed her strong desire to meet her goal of earning a PhD and promised them she would be more attentive to family. They made arrangements to Skype every weekend. They also booked airplane tickets for the holidays. This made everyone more relaxed knowing they would soon be together again.

I was proud of Shelley for turning things around. She became a model student who helped other incoming students learn to adapt to the demands of graduate school. Shelley went on to successfully graduate with her PhD. She called me recently to tell me about her new assistant professor position. Shelley was happy to report that she was limiting her activities and is now focused on improving her teaching and research skills. I felt glad that I could help a good student get over the initial hurdles to her success in graduate school.

→

Kathy goes on to tell about another student with a different set of issues, in this case related to being a first-time college instructor as a graduate teaching assistant. When his job as a TA presented him with some difficult issues, Richard made the wise decision to see Kathy for advice.

LESSONS LEARNED AS A TEACHING ASSISTANT

Kathy: Most of the graduate students who come to talk to me have never been teachers. Often their first teaching experiences are filled with surprises. Sometimes they are nervous, and most of the time they have interactions with undergraduates that produce questions they would not have expected.

During the spring semester, Richard, a teaching assistant in sociology, came to my office. He was teaching an introductory sociology course and was having unexpected challenges. He had already been a teaching assistant in the fall so he was not overly concerned with organizing the content of the course. Instead he was focused on one particular student. Richard was frustrated because he had a student who seemed to be having difficulties comprehending what he read and who had difficulty following instructions. However, his student seemed to be very intelligent, caught onto new ideas easily, and participated eloquently in class discussions.

I asked Richard to tell me more about the situation but to keep the student's name to himself to protect the student's privacy. Richard said he really felt he needed to talk to someone but was afraid that if he went to someone in his department, they would identify the student. I reassured him that I would hold everything in confidence and pointed out that I did not work with undergraduate students in the sociology department.

Richard then began to tell his story. To respect confidentiality, he called his student "Chris," whom he said was very vocal in class. In fact, he reminded Richard of the class clown from high school. All the other students laughed when Chris would speak out and make comments in class. Richard sometimes found his behavior disruptive, but there were numerous times when his comments were very insightful. Richard's feelings about Chris were mixed. He was irritated when Chris was disrupting class, but felt gratified when Chris's comments made other students stop and reflect on the topics being discussed.

Richard liked to use active learning techniques in his classroom that promoted student involvement. He often had the students work in groups and present their work to their classmates. Chris was very popular. Most of the other students liked having him in their group. The first issue arose, however, when the class groups were required to read materials from the textbook, and then as a group create a presentation based on the topic. Chris had a difficult time remembering what he had read the night before. When the material was discussed in the group he did fine. When he had to recall information on his own, however, issues arose. His group discussed their project in class, and then each member was expected to create three to four PowerPoint slides for the presentation the next day. Each group would receive a grade on participation points. The group members would rate each other, and then Richard would assign an overall grade for the presentation. Chris received very poor grades from his teammates. His team as a whole received a "B-." Several of his group members complained to Richard. They felt they had done their part and their work deserved a higher grade. They did not feel their grade should be impacted because of what they perceived as Chris's inability to deliver effective PowerPoint slides.

The second indication Richard had that Chris was struggling was the first quiz. Chris came to talk to Richard during class office hours about the upcoming quiz. Richard talked with him at length about various concepts that were discussed in class, and Chris seemed to comprehend the topics. Richard liked Chris and felt confident that he would do well on the upcoming quiz, especially after their long discussion. The next day during the quiz, Richard observed Chris's behavior. Every time he looked at him, Chris was staring out the window or playing with his watch. Chris was the last one to finish the quiz. Richard was disappointed when he graded Chris's work. He had missed over half the questions. How could Chris be so knowledgeable when he was discussing the topics and still receive a "D" on his quiz?

Finally, the incident that led Richard to my door involved an observation assignment. Richard wanted his students to practice a social science research method that involved direct observation. The techniques for the assignment were handed out in class. The class was divided into groups, and the group members were each assigned to choose one individual to observe in the student union. They were all expected to describe the environment in detail, including a drawing of the surroundings. This would include describing anything in the environment that could possibly affect the person's behavior, such as windows, doors, seating arrangements, people, and lighting. Then they were to record a detailed description of their subject's behavior, minute by minute. Their observation was to last five minutes. When they were done, they were to return to class and were instructed to compare notes among the group members. Finally, they were asked to complete a similar observation, on their own, as a homework assignment.

Chris seemed to do well with the classroom assignment. However, the next day when Richard checked his mailbox, he found a sheet of paper that was incomprehensible. It appeared to be written in a stream of consciousness writing style. Richard started to throw the sheet of paper in the trash bin, but something made him stop and take a closer look. He noticed Chris's name in the upper right-hand corner. Richard looked again at the content of the writing. It described an incident that took place on campus, a girl going outside to have a cigarette. The writing didn't make clear sense, and to Richard it seemed as if Chris had written a complaint of noncompliance with the new campus smoke-free environment policy. However, after reexamination, Richard realized it was Chris's homework assignment. It did not resemble the descriptive observation that was required for the assignment. The inconsistency between the performance Chris demonstrated in class as part of the group practice session and his individual performance on the homework assignment baffled Richard.

Richard told me that he thought Chris might have a disability. I asked him if Chris had been officially identified as having a disability and he replied that he had not. But Richard didn't want to see Chris fail. We discussed the need for Chris to go to the Disability Resource Center (DRC) to be tested for a disability and discussed options available to instructors when a student has not identified his or her disability. I explained to Richard that the DRC would provide information on how to be compliant with federal regulations. We made an appointment for the following week.

When Richard returned, he told me that Chris had once again come to his class office hours. Chris was stressed about his performance on the quiz and the observation assignment. He then admitted to Richard that in grade school he had been identified with attention deficit hyperactivity disorder (ADHD); he also had a learning disability. Chris had dealt with disability issues all through his elementary school years. He was finally diagnosed and received help in high school. But he had not wanted to be labeled with a disability in college. He felt that everyone would treat him differently. He did not want his professors to judge him based on his disabilities.

Richard referred Chris to the DRC. Since this was the first time Richard had worked with a student who had a disability, he was nervous that he might not be able to adapt his teaching to fit the required accommodations. But things worked out. Chris received help with his writing assignments; he had a scribe come to his classes with him to take notes. At first he was embarrassed to have a scribe go to class with him, but after a couple of weeks the difference it made was worth any embarrassment he initially felt.

Chris also was provided with a computer software program that allowed him to talk out his ideas. The program learned his voice and translated it into a written document. What a difference it made for Chris to be able to talk through his ideas, have them translated into a written document, and not lose information. Finally, Chris was allowed to take all of his exams in a separate room. This helped with the distractions and allotted him more time to take the exams. Again, Chris was concerned that other students would notice and make fun of him for the special arrangements. But his classmates were worried about their own performance; they never asked Chris where he was on exam days.

The following year I ran into Richard at a graduation event. He was happy to see me and told me that spring semester had been a real learning experience for him. He was thrilled that Chris had endured and succeeded in his class and had turned out to be one of his top students. He had seen Chris recently and said he was doing well in his coursework and was well on track to graduating. Richard told me that after the experience with Chris, he made sure he was aware of all the support programs on campus and asked his department mentors if they could make a resource list for all new teaching assistants so that they would be well informed and able to help their students with special needs.

My experience with Richard and the effort he put into helping Chris succeed is an example of how campus support programs can help graduate students meet their teaching and research challenges. These programs are designed to be there for graduate students and, as I have often seen, they can make the positive difference in their success.

MANAGING RESEARCH RESPONSIBILITIES

Even more central than teaching responsibilities, a graduate student's scholarship is at the heart of the graduate degree. Cyndi relates her experience working with students who encountered some barriers on the research leg of their graduate journey. These barriers are often associated with common transitions encountered in graduate education, such as the transition from coursework to the research lab, managing multiple assistantships, or the transition from the research lab to writing the dissertation.

Cyndi: Nothing is more fulfilling than hearing the success stories of students whom I have helped make their way through difficulties in graduate school. The next narrative is about two students who stopped me on campus and told me how they used strategies learned in professional development workshops they had attended on campus to overcome a major crisis and improve their performance in their research lab. They told me how they did this in detail.

Mason, a third-year graduate student, had recently finished his coursework, which allowed him to devote his full attention to his research. However, his research advisor, Dr. Cooper, recently had cut Mason's research assistantship from half-time to quarter-time in order to provide funding for Talia, who had lost her half-time teaching assistantship as a result of departmental budget cuts. Then Dr. Cooper left for two weeks to attend out-of-town conferences. Concerned about the decrease in his income and the impact on his benefits such as medical insurance, Mason applied for and received a quarter-time research assistantship in Dr. Agrawal's lab. The research in Dr. Agrawal's lab was intriguing, and Mason enjoyed the climate of the lab and interactions with his fellow researchers. As the semester progressed, the research activities in Dr. Agrawal's lab advanced rapidly. Mason spent more and more time there, but in Dr. Cooper's lab he encountered several challenges with his research to the point that this research stalled and he was completely neglecting his own dissertation project. He had asked Talia, the fifth-year graduate student in Dr. Cooper's lab, for help, but she was too busy with her own activities. Dr. Cooper had said that the data and methods were needed by mid-semester to write and submit the proposal to continue the grant, which was the source of funding for Mason's assistantship. To add to his stress, Dr. Cooper e-mailed Mason wanting to meet on Monday to discuss the data collected, results obtained, and progress Mason had made. Mason did not have any data or results and had not made any progress. What was he going to do? At this rate, he felt like he would never finish his dissertation.

At the same time Mason was having his difficulties, Talia was overwhelmed and frustrated. As a fifth-year graduate student, she was entering the job market, intent on obtaining a faculty position in a prestigious liberal arts college that valued teaching and undergraduate research. She had been fortunate to secure funding each semester as a research assistant for Dr. Cooper. During the previous spring semester, to enhance her teaching portfolio, she had requested and received a half-time teaching assistantship to teach two courses in the fall. With her research progressing so well, her goal was to focus on developing her teaching portfolio, and perhaps even conduct a study of teaching and learning and submit a journal article as she had learned about in the Preparing Future Faculty course she had taken last spring. Talia had identified a teaching mentor, Dr. Walls, a faculty member in the college who had received recognition and awards for his teaching activities and had published extensively on his scholarship of teaching. However, it seemed like her dream was rapidly crumbling at her feet.

Two weeks before the semester started, the graduate chair had cut her teaching assistantship back from two courses to one. Fortunately, Dr. Cooper had saved the day and continued her research assistantship as a quarter-time appointment. She would manage the lab, mentor Mason, and teach Dr. Cooper's introductory course since he was traveling extensively during the semester. Initially, Talia was honored that Dr. Cooper entrusted these responsibilities to her, but now everything was in dreadful chaos. Teaching the course required much more time than she had anticipated, although she had faithfully attended several teaching workshops and she and Dr. Walls had detailed a teaching development plan in conjunction with a plan she created after attending a professional development workshop on individual development plans. Initially she was accomplishing all of her the goals and completing her tasks. Her plan kept her on task, on time, and focused on her priorities. But now, her teaching and managing the lab consumed much more of her time than she had anticipated, particularly since Mason had been mysteriously missing in action for the past few weeks. Talia knew that Mason was struggling with some of his experiments and had sought her advice a week or so back, but she did not have time to meet with him and review his methods and data. Talia herself had not conducted any of her own experiments over the past few weeks and was starting to run dangerously behind on everything. One afternoon when she was reading her e-mail and thinking things could not be worse, a message popped up from Dr. Cooper, who was back from his latest trip and wanted to meet on Monday to discuss the lab activities and research results. What was she going to do? It was Friday and she had nothing to report!

Talia took several deep breaths to quell the panic attack that washed over her, then she pondered her options. She did not know where to begin. The whole situation was overwhelming, reminiscent of how she felt when she began writing her dissertation. She decided to use one of the approaches she had learned in the dissertation writing strategies workshop she had attended a few months earlier. Talia focused on establishing a deadline, Monday in this case, and identifying attainable goals. What could she accomplish in two days? What would have the biggest impact? Since time was short, she focused on three goals: get Mason refocused on his research, work with Mason on a mentoring plan that would benefit both of them, and develop a research plan for her work in the lab similar to her teaching plan. While she knew Dr. Cooper would be disappointed in her lack of research results, she and Mason would have strong plans for moving forward. After e-mailing Mason to meet her in the lab at 10:00 on Saturday morning, Talia quickly finished her grading and hurried home. She wanted to get to the lab early on Saturday to organize the research activities and mentoring materials prior to Mason's arrival.

Mason, in the meantime, was relieved to see the e-mail from Talia. She was intelligent, very skilled in the lab, and initially had been a great mentor by helping him get started in the lab. He was eager to discuss his research issues and get back on track before meeting with Dr. Cooper. Attached to her e-mail were mentoring resources, including "How to Create Your Research Agenda," "Communicating with Your Advisor," and "How to Be Productive, Not Busy—Time Management Tips," handouts that Talia had received when she attended a mentoring workshop earlier in the semester. She asked Mason to review the resources, and to identify mentoring goals and issues so they could develop a mentoring plan for the rest of the semester that would align with both of their research activities and goals. They met early on Saturday morning. They scheduled weekly lab meetings on their calendars along with times when both would be in the lab working. This schedule was important since both had other assistantships and associated responsibilities. Next, they tackled the research agenda, complete with timelines for abstracts, conferences, and funding proposals, which they would present to Dr. Cooper for his input. Finally, they worked together to identify the issues with Mason's research. Once all of the goals were revised and accomplished, they both felt a sense of accomplishment. Although they had not met the originals goals established by Dr. Cooper, Talia and Mason worked together and regrouped, meeting the demands of their multiple assistantship responsibilities.

When Talia and Mason met with Dr. Cooper, they explained the issues they had each encountered in their research. Next they listed the steps in their research agenda for accomplishing the goals set forth by Dr. Cooper and asked for his feedback. While Dr. Cooper was obviously disappointed with their lack of progress, he was impressed with their initiative in identifying solutions to resolve their research issues.

Presenting workshops to help graduate students succeed in their work is very rewarding, but actually hearing about how two students had applied the techniques I presented was an amazing experience. As I listened to Talia and Mason recount their story to me, I could see how pleased they were with their progress, and how happy they were to be moving toward their goals in their respective programs. I felt very proud of them as students because they have dealt with the responsibilities of graduate assistantships in a mature and organized fashion.

CONCLUSION

The narratives we have presented here demonstrate some of the issues graduate students encounter in their multiple roles as student, academician, scholar, and colleague. Reaching out to other students, faculty, and staff in your graduate program and across campus, along with tapping into the other suggested support services, can help you develop a network of colleagues and accumulate skills, which will serve you long after you complete your PhD.

CHAPTER 8 GROUP DISCUSSION

While graduate school provides the setting for academic learning, it also can challenge you to learn about yourself and your limitations. As Cyndi and Kathy have expressed in this chapter, graduate students can come up against circumstances that go beyond their knowledge, in which case it is up to them to reach out to the various support services and networks available on campus. Ironically, oftentimes those who need help the most are those who do not seek it out.

This problem of adequately recognizing one's problems and making the decision to seek support is the topic of the video for this chapter. The video, titled *The Choice*, and accompanying materials for leading a group discussion can be downloaded from the chapter 8 resource web page at http://dx.doi.org/10.5703/1288284315206.

CHAPTER AUTHOR PROFILES

Cyndi Lynch

Ms. Lynch is the director of fellowships and graduate student professional development for the Purdue University Graduate School. She is a registered veterinary technician, focusing on animal behavior. Ms. Lynch holds a BS degree in animal science and an MS degree in curriculum and instruction from Purdue University. Her research focuses on doctoral student engagement and the assessment of doctoral student learning outcomes in identified best practices, including mentoring, developing effective writing strategies, orientations and transition courses, and doctoral student professional development. Ms. Lynch administers Purdue's Preparing Future Faculty and Preparing Future Professionals courses.

Kathy Garza Dixon, PhD

Dr. Dixon is the program director for the Alliance for Graduate Education and the Professoriate (AGEP) and the co-director of the Summer Research Opportunities Program (SROP) at Purdue University. She focuses on the recruitment, retention, and enrichment of underrepresented graduate students and provides support for postdocs seeking positions in academia. Dr. Dixon received her BA degree in psychology and her PhD in educational psychology with a concentration in human development from Indiana University. Prior to joining AGEP, Dr. Dixon served as the program director for a Lilly endowment grant at Ancilla College, where she taught psychology and developed recruitment, transition, retention, and diversity programs to support nontraditional and underrepresented college students. Dr. Dixon also worked as a visiting professor at Indiana University Southeast, where she taught courses in human development, education, and psychology. She is committed to increasing and supporting diversity in higher education. Her research interest is based on a multidisciplinary developmental approach to understanding the belief systems and academic achievement of minority college students.

Chapter 9

Publishing While Completing the PhD

G. Leah Davis, PhD

INTRODUCTION

In academia, the saying "publish or perish" is often used to describe the arduous process of publishing to gain tenure as a professor. Even earlier, however, having a published article often opens doors when graduate students go on the job market. Opportunities for employment can be missed if the newly minted PhD does not have at least a few publications listed on her or his curriculum vitae. The question is, in the face of the rigorous demands of graduate studies and teaching responsibilities, how can a graduate student also research, write, and publish quality work? The answer to this question is as varied as the graduate students who pursue this goal, as the opportunities to publish during graduate school present themselves in different places and in various ways.

In this chapter, I relate the steps I took in order to get published before I graduated, including two methods that are very common and one that is a little unconventional. My experiences in pursuing these publication projects were often challenging and suspenseful, but in the end, fully worth the effort, which the stories below describe. You will see how going the extra mile and getting published while still in your PhD program is possible and can give you the publications you will need in order to compete in the job market successfully.

AN OVERVIEW OF THE GRADUATE STUDENT PUBLICATION CHALLENGE

According to several experts in the field of higher education, research needs to be driven by intrinsic motivation and the belief that one can accomplish one's goals, rather than finding motivation solely in the external pressures to publish. I found working on a group project was a very good way to stimulate my inner motivation in the face of the external pressure to get that first publication. Graduate student colleagues can collaborate as a research team that writes an article, report, or a contribution to a conference proceeding publication. The team members divide the tasks for the research project, which lessens the stress of taking on an entire project on one's own. In addition, research has shown that scholarly and intellectual writing is developed positively through social engagement. A research team provides a social outlet to conceive original research topics, expand on good ideas, and write innovatively.

In terms of writing and publishing an actual article, one way to learn this process is through an academic apprenticeship, where the PhD student is mentored by a professor who provides guidance throughout the publication process. The outcome of this collaboration is generally a publication in a scholarly journal. A good mentor will provide high-level instruction *and* encourage the development of quality research and writing skills needed for academic publishing. Another path to publishing during graduate school is presenting a research paper at a professional conference and then having your paper included in the conference proceedings. This approach can be very rewarding, especially if it is done with a colleague or faculty mentor, or both, as you also learn how to prepare research for a professional presentation for scholars from all over the country and internationally. Still other opportunities to publish can be found, such as contributing to a chapter in a book, writing a review of a new book in your field, preparing articles for professional newsletters, contributing to a serial publication, writing and moderating a blog on the web, or writing a feature article for a newspaper. I relate next how, while in graduate school, I started my curriculum vitae publications list. The process was not painless, but it was worth it.

MY PATH TO PUBLICATION AS A GRADUATE STUDENT

Facing the publish or perish dragon and learning the ropes of the academic publishing process was something I definitely did not want to put off until I had graduated. I knew that the successful researcher is measured not only by her or his competence in rigorous academic research, but also by the ability to publish research findings in professional journals. Moreover, manuscripts selected for publication contain findings that contribute to existing knowledge and advance the field in new and innovative ways. Could I possibly achieve this goal while still in graduate school? Over the years of my graduate school experience, I learned that the road to publishing can be daunting for a PhD student, but what I learned over time with different publication experiences was well worth the effort. I also learned that I could pursue several avenues that would teach me how to conduct quality research, write scholarly articles, and begin a publication record while in graduate school, all prior to going out into the job market.

I first established my research publication record when a group of classmates and I responded to our professor's suggestion that we work together on a publication for a top-tier journal. I then had the opportunity to collaborate with a professor on a peer-reviewed journal article, and later I worked on a research project with a colleague and we presented our results at a professional conference with the plan to publish our paper in the conference proceedings. Here is my story.

My First Venture: Group Collaboration

In the spring of 2002, about a month into the second semester of my PhD program, I took a seminar on the management of nonprofit organizations. The professor, Dr. Cheswick, challenged a group of my classmates and me to take advantage of an opportunity to publish in *ARNOVA Abstracts*, a quarterly publication of the Association for Research on Nonprofit Organizations and Voluntary Action (ARNOVA), the leading international research association of the nonprofit sector. In addition to publishing scholarly articles in its premier journal, *Nonprofit and Voluntary Sector Quarterly*, ARNOVA publishes abstracts for articles published on a variety of topics about nonprofit organizations. Dr. Cheswick encouraged us: "I want you to learn the steps to getting published. I will provide you with guidance, but this is your project from beginning to end." She explained that we would be responsible for researching, writing, and editing an issue for this journal. Even though this publication did not require peer review, it nonetheless offered an excellent venue for our publication efforts.

My colleagues and I were very excited about this opportunity, and we agreed with Dr. Cheswick that it would be a great way to acquaint ourselves with submitting written work to a journal. We were an eclectic group of people with varied academic interests in public affairs: two in public management (including me), three in public finance, and two in political science. Regardless of our varying specializations, we approached our publication project as a team. One of our colleagues, Tim, was appointed as group leader to keep everyone on task. The first step involved the review of current and back issues of *ARNOVA Abstracts*. In our discussion of the abstracts, we came up with the idea to organize the articles we would read around a particular theme. Although the journal issues called for abstracts of specific articles, we decided to present a "theme" idea to the ARNOVA editor for a special edition. We also knew that determining a gap in the literature was important, and we found that little work had been done on the unethical or controversial policies, practices, and outcomes of nonprofit organizations. So we settled on the topic "the dark side of nonprofit organizations" for the theme of our abstract research. The next week we contacted the journal editor with our topic idea. We also asked for permission to serve as guest editors for this particular edition. Tim was our contact person. All we could do was wait for the ARNOVA editor's reply—a very nerve-wracking process.

During this waiting time, we were very excited because we were fully invested in our project for the journal, but we were also nervous because we didn't know if our proposal would be accepted. A very long and dreary two weeks went by in February until one day Tim came into class, and we could tell by the smile on his face that he had received good news. The ARNOVA editor had finally responded and agreed to let us serve as guest editors. She said she liked our idea to organize our abstracts around the theme of the dark side of nonprofit organizations. We all cheered when we got this news from Tim and then immediately got to work.

The editor had given us guidelines for writing the abstracts and the submission time frame, with the admonition that it was important that we stay on schedule. The following week in class, each group member took on the task of reviewing currently published abstracts to learn the appropriate tone and style, as well as the format for the abstracts we had to write. Next, we developed five categories for the various types of published and unpublished research materials we would study for unethical behaviors in nonprofit organizations: journal articles, news articles, dissertations, books, and working papers. Two of my colleagues and I were charged with reviewing and writing abstracts about research articles published in journals on nonprofit organizations. We also had to concern ourselves with making sure that the content, attributions, and references in everyone's abstracts were all correct and followed ARNOVA's style guide. Two group members were responsible for collecting the abstracts and merging them into one document. Added to this, we had the task of editing our final document for technical errors. Another group member wrote the cover letter. Everyone involved worked regularly on his or her contribution, and during the seventh week of the project, we submitted the completed abstracts on time to the ARNOVA editor.

We all felt greatly relieved when it was clear that we had met the March 31 deadline and the project had turned out well. Winter was also turning into warmer spring days, so we all shed our winter moods and went out for pizza to celebrate. Then, the next milestone came when Tim arrived in class with the news that our work had been accepted and a special abstracts edition would be published in the subsequent fall issue of *ARNOVA Abstracts*. After a typically sweltering Indiana summer, September finally arrived, and with it, the new edition of *ARNOVA Abstracts* containing our project, finally published! And, amazing as it was to me, there stood my name in print along with the rest of my graduate school colleagues. Our smiles and satisfaction lit up our lab with enthusiasm.

With the completion of this first group publication, I felt like I was well on my way to working on an actual article myself. Through this project, I had learned to focus and organize a research topic and to collaborate with a group in a disciplined way. I began to learn and understand the importance of balancing publishing projects that require a high level of excellence while maintaining a similarly high level of achievement in my own coursework and classroom teaching. Although this project was relatively small, it had shown me that the publication process was not so easy, and that in order to gain tenure, life as a professor would require a great deal of time dedicated to research in order to develop and publish credible work. At some point most students begin to understand the hard work that is required to publish in the academy, and for me, this understanding began with the ARNOVA project. I was successful in my endeavor, so I remain glad that I had the courage to take Dr. Cheswick's advice and embrace this project. It helped me realize that I could manage the publishing task well and actually get to see my name in print!

Our group publication experience familiarized all of us with the manifold aspects of publishing. Along with learning how to identify a gap in the literature, we discovered that other publication venues would be interested in articles from us on this subject that went well beyond what was written in the nonprofit journals. The process of writing the abstracts proved to be very instrumental in identifying a potentially new research area for cross-disciplinary research in the nonprofit sector, which really excited and inspired me as well as the entire group! My first experience as a productive and published writer had put me on the way to establishing a solid research and publication record while I was completing my PhD program. The next step was to work on an actual peer-reviewed journal article, and just such an opportunity came my way not too long after we published the *ARNOVA Abstracts* special edition issue. Fortunately, I had the courage to step up to this challenge and the perseverance to get through it successfully.

Coauthoring with an Advisor or Faculty Member

Another avenue to publishing while in graduate school is to collaborate on a peer-reviewed journal article with a faculty mentor. This type of peer-reviewed journal article writing experience is one of the most common and best ways for graduate students to break into publishing. A graduate student can learn a great deal from the expertise and knowledge of a tenured faculty mentor who has published in many journals. Collaboration on academic writing with a seasoned career professional can invoke real or imagined pressures to write in a scholarly style that meets the expectations and external standards of one's professors, one's colleagues, and the field as a whole. This type of interaction can trigger inner turmoil, pessimistic thoughts, and feelings of inadequacy about one's academic capabilities, but the learning process one goes through in coping with these challenges is well worth the effort.

My next story shows how I faced the challenge of writing and publishing a journal article with my advisor in my minor area of study, business, while balancing graduate level coursework. My advisor provided me with supervision to keep the research project on task from inception to publication, but I also had to overcome conflict with my advisor, which I was able to do with the help of a colleague and friend who provided me with scholarly advice and collegial support. I learned that diffusing negative or confrontational interactions with a professor is critical to the preservation of one's reputation as a student who can do quality work and balance a full academic schedule.

During the third year of my PhD program, one afternoon I found myself hurrying to the Kelley School of Business to meet with Dr. Rosen, my minor program advisor. He had sent me an e-mail the week before to schedule a meeting, and now the day to meet with him had arrived. I walked down the brightly lit hallway to his office. The eclectic mix of colorful photographs and postcards from Africa and other countries posted on his door, I was to learn, reflected his many-sided personality. I knocked, and after a moment he opened the door, invited me in, greeted me with a warm smile, and said, "Hello, how are you doing?" "Great!" I responded as I sat down and then noticed his smile had changed. He was giving me a rather serious look. He asked, "How would you like to publish an article in the *Academy of Management Journal* with me?" A big smile spread across my face, and I said without hesitation, "Oh, yes, I would!" Dr. Rosen welcomed my enthusiasm. I tried not to show it, but I felt slightly stunned. Thoughts about my current situation began to run through my mind. I was studying for my public management qualifying exam, which I was scheduled to take in the summer, and I was completing coursework in preparation for this exam. I felt pretty sure I could manage it all though. How could I say no to Dr. Rosen and an opportunity like this?

I was elated with this invitation to work with him on an article for *The Academy of Management*, a top-tier, peer-reviewed journal in the business field. I regarded this as the opportunity of a lifetime, and one of the primary goals of any PhD student who wants to pursue a career in academia. It is true that, as a graduate student, I could approach my professors about publication projects as well, but to have a faculty member ask me, this was a real honor. Dr. Rosen then said that another student whom he was advising, Lisa, would also be working on the project. I knew Lisa and got along well with her, so I was very happy to hear that she was also included on the project. Dr. Rosen told me he would send an e-mail to set a meeting with Lisa and me the following week to discuss the details of the article. I left his office still smiling and walked out of the building into the cool, sunny day that perfectly reflected my mood.

Our meeting was set for the following week in the conference room in the Kelley School. I saw Lisa coming down the hall, and we walked into the conference room together. Dr. Rosen was already there, seated and ready to begin the meeting. He began by saying that he would be first author, Lisa would be second, and I would be third. This position as last did not change my mind about the project. I was just excited to be included in the collaboration and given the opportunity to publish in a top-tier business journal. An established publication record was very important to me and would greatly strengthen my curriculum vitae. Although this would be my second publication, I did not have one that was peer reviewed. Moreover, I believed that writing this article would prove fruitful for a possible dissertation topic where I could potentially combine my public management major and business minor.

As the meeting progressed, we used the chalkboard to brainstorm and narrow down our research ideas. It was interesting that our ideas converged in the areas of information technology and business. We decided to write an article reviewing the state of electronic commerce in the United States and international supply chain management. Dr. Rosen was responsible for overseeing the project. He agreed to write the introduction, background, and conclusion. Lisa volunteered to review the literature on the topic written by international researchers. I took on the responsibility of reviewing and writing about the literature by US scholars. I knew the corpus of literature was large, but believed I could handle the workload. The three of us agreed to collaborate on writing the recommendations for future research. At the conclusion of our meeting, we established a one-month deadline for the literature review, and we also agreed to meet weekly to discuss our progress.

The very next day after our meeting I began to work on the literature review. I learned very quickly that this project was a lot more time consuming and taxing than I had expected because not only did I have to read sixty-plus articles in order to decide which ones would not be included in the manuscript, I also had to conduct a content analysis of the articles to be included. Twenty-three articles met the criteria for inclusion, and I entered the data from the content analysis on a spreadsheet for further analysis. These tasks were just the beginning of the project however, and I was starting to feel the strain of what was becoming a very burdensome workload.

In addition, Dr. Rosen was highly meticulous and demanding. His impatience and his perfectionism made working with him very intense. I had experienced these traits of his before while taking several of his graduate courses. His often difficult behavior was a well-worn topic of conversation with some graduate students in the department who thought he mistreated students and was unfair, even though at other times he could be very congenial. In addition to Dr. Rosen's over-the-top personality and working to meet the deadline of the manuscript, the quickly approaching day of my scheduled qualifying exam loomed ahead of me like a dark cloud. I had to balance this huge load, and my stress level intensified with each passing day as I tried my best to keep up with all the work the project involved. Then during our third meeting three weeks after the project began, Dr. Rosen's tone of voice became a little heated, and he began to question the number of articles that I had reviewed and if I had sufficiently read and analyzed them. I knew that he was questioning my ability to do the work. This publication was very important to Dr. Rosen; many of his colleagues would see his name on it in a highly read, top-tier business journal. I didn't want to let him down or embarrass him, so I sat there, silent and intimidated, not sure how to respond to a professor who showed negative emotions, since I had never been in this collaborative situation with him before. However, I was also feeling very frustrated with him because he was expecting me to be perfect at something I had never done before. If I needed some help, why didn't he just offer it, or advise me on what to do to improve?

I had heard from others in my program that the graduate student code of behavior when working with a professor is to go along with the program and appease him or her to get the publication out and to protect your name and reputation in the department. So, as I reflected on my situation, I decided in our next meeting to assure Dr. Rosen that I was on task with the literature I was reviewing given our criteria. We met in the afternoon on a Friday, and I was extra tired and pretty stressed, but I managed to show a positive attitude during the meeting. Fortunately, my coauthor and colleague, Lisa, picked up on my actual demeanor, the slightly unsure look on my face, and the fact that I was anxious about the situation. Dr. Rosen began to review my work with a measured and critical tone; Lisa immediately interjected and told Dr. Rosen that my work was coming along fine and she would follow up with me. Since Lisa and Dr. Rosen had worked together before, he calmed down and agreed with her. After we left the meeting, she encouraged me by saying things would be okay and reemphasized that Dr. Rosen was a perfectionist. His critical tone was part of his personality, and I should not take his behavior too personally. She offered to come to my home to assist me and to ensure that I was on the right track with my section of the review and other work on the article. I said yes to her idea, and the discouragement that I was feeling began to lift. I was thankful that she extended her help to me. I hadn't been aware that I might need assistance to ensure that my work was on track, and unfortunately, I learned that this was indeed the case through the negative interaction with Dr. Rosen. His unsupportive attitude bothered me somewhat. I felt as if I were being held accountable for something Dr. Rosen should have anticipated and followed up on, or made clear from the beginning of this project.

The same week, Lisa came over to my home and reviewed my work with me. She gave me some pointers on how to get the review done more quickly and to ensure its accuracy. Lisa was further along in her PhD program and had prior experience publishing. I was very grateful for her valuable examples and advice, and I even began to adopt her apparently effortless writing style, as I was still refining my own. With Lisa's help, I gained the confidence I needed to carry out the project and completed my portion of the work. Thanks to her help, Dr. Rosen was pleased with my work, and I no longer was the target of his dissatisfaction and anger.

The work then picked up speed, and after the usual edits and reedits, the labor we had put into this project started to bear fruit. Our article was published, and we received invitations to present our research at the Kelley School. Other invitations came to us to share our research in the United States and internationally. My advisor even traveled to Europe to present our research at a conference, which greatly inspired me and made me realize that one day I would be presenting my own research in similar venues.

The success of our collaboration and article hinged on diffusing the potentially volatile situation between my faculty advisor and me. Looking back on it, I can see now that as I got into the project I needed direction; as a first-time author there were some things that I simply needed to learn. My advisor's impatient communication style exacerbated the situation. If I had relied on his help to mentor me, his negative communications could have impeded the progress on our article and tarnished my reputation in the department.

I had learned a valuable lesson: I could turn to someone else for the help I needed, which I learned to do in this project. By being open and accepting the much-needed help from my colleague, although my need for this help was unexpected, I found that I could successfully complete my part of the project and make a valuable contribution to the article. Had I not reacted carefully to the negative situation with Dr. Rosen and said yes to my colleague's help, Dr. Rosen might have removed me from the project. I never would have succeeded in this opportunity of a lifetime to participate in writing a prestigious peer-reviewed article for a major publication in my field while still a PhD student. I knew that I could contribute to an article for publication with a lot of hard work, and by remaining true to myself and keeping my eye on the prize, I did fulfill my advisor's expectations of me as well as my expectations of myself. And so I succeeded in the end. The experience on the whole was very positive. It gave me the courage to take on my next publication adventure, which involved a collaborative project with a fellow graduate student.

The Independent Research Project and Conference Presentation

With the success of two published articles under my belt, I felt quite ready to accept the next opportunity for publishing. This time I was looking at a slightly unconventional option in publishing at the graduate student level: the initiation of an independent research project in collaboration with a graduate student colleague and the scholarly presentation of our findings, followed up with an attempt to publish our article. My next story relates a similar type of experience, only this one also involves the difficulties that can occur when a professor or mentor does not provide adequate consultation for an independent research project.

I need to say in advance that only graduate students who are far enough along in their PhD program so that they have learned the skills needed to effectively manage this type of research and its scholarly presentation are advised to take on such a project. It demands a strong focus on one's work and much dedication—challenges that I definitely encountered when I embarked on this independent research project in collaboration with my graduate student colleague. Also, the oversight of a faculty advisor when undertaking independent research is advisable, even though it is not officially required. Although we had very little of it, faculty guidance can be very helpful to ensure that the research is being conducted properly and that it will successfully obtain valid and reliable findings that contribute to the field. Regarding funding, a research grant typically provides funding for a faculty member and graduate students to conduct research. It is often expected by the funding agency that the researchers present and publish their findings. In our case, we were able to complete our research project while in graduate school without outside funding, and we also were able to seek out a conference where we could present our findings, although we had no guarantee that they would be published. My colleague's and my experience in taking the risk to pursue research on our own taught us many of the ins and outs of the research process and coauthoring an article for publication.

My story begins with my colleague, Michelle, who had organized a support group in our department to develop closer working relationships between minority PhD students in order to foster academic collaboration for research, publishing, and other academic endeavors important to completing a PhD. Our department had very few minorities, and we did not always feel as if we were being supported as up-and-coming scholars or that our research ideas were respected. This support group proved to fulfill its mission very well and helped several of us gain confidence and move forward in our graduate studies. It very much served to bring Michelle and me together to work on our idea for an independent research project.

In the spring semester, during one of our monthly meetings, Michelle and I decided to research how nonprofit organizations use technology to accomplish organizational tasks and meet their strategic goals. We wanted to publish our findings, and this meant that we had decided to conduct our own original research, even though we didn't have any funding or a committed faculty mentor to turn to for advice along the way. Little did we know that we had gotten ourselves into a project more difficult than we expected, and so we proceeded unhesitatingly with our plan. We set our goals: first, to present our research at a major conference in our field held by the Association for Public Policy Analysis and Management (APPAM), and second, to submit our conference paper for publication.

Michelle and I decided that we would conduct three case studies in different Indiana cities looking at nonprofit organizations and their use of technology. First, we wrote the abstract, which we collaborated on, and then submitted it to APPAM for review. About three months later we were both elated to learn that our abstract had been accepted. This particular conference has a reputation for rigorous, high-quality presentations, so our research idea must have been very good in order for the abstract to be accepted, which was quite an accomplishment. The quality that APPAM demands of presentations is correspondingly rigorous. Consequently, the PhD students who present at

APPAM usually do so with a professor because few graduate students are capable of meeting APPAM's high standards.

This is not to say that we did not try to find a faculty mentor to advise us. I had approached a professor in our department, Dr. Engley, whose area of research dovetailed with our project's topic. I felt the need and the professional responsibility to check our idea with her to see if she thought it was a viable research area. When we spoke, however, Dr. Engley was very unhelpful. She was quite negative about our research project, told me that we didn't really need a research question to proceed, and posed several questions to me that were confusing and threatened to obscure the direction we were going with our research idea. I was rather surprised, if not shocked, at her response to our initiative; it was disappointing at best, and at worst, undermining. The suggestion that we not develop a research question seemed almost irrational and went against everything I had been taught about research. During our conversation, I was polite and did my best to remain objective and collegial, but I was glad when our conversation was finished.

At that point, we could have continued trying to work out our idea with Dr. Engley, but since I had voluntarily asked her for help, I felt okay about continuing the project without her. Looking back on it, this was the best decision we could have made under the circumstances. Fortunately, neither Michelle nor I was in a class with Dr. Engley or had her as an advisor. Although we were not completely happy about it, we quietly decided to proceed on our own and did not seek out another mentor. This meant that we were headed into some demanding territory unawares, the consequences of which we felt when it came time to publish our work. But more on that later.

After our abstract had been accepted by APPAM, we focused on the next step of our research. Michelle and I had to complete the application for human subjects review. We agreed that I would serve as the principal investigator for our project. The human subjects review was a tedious process, but I made sure our application was thorough and covered the necessary documentation, including a summary of our research design, sampling methodology, and data collection instrument. Much to my surprise, only two weeks after we had submitted our application we were granted human subjects approval. I felt empowered because I was experiencing the research process on my own without help from a professor. The successful steps along the way to starting our research, which included our abstract submission and acceptance and a quick human subjects approval (usually a longer process), helped me to feel confident that we really could complete this research project. These successes added up to a life-changing moment for me as a developing researcher. I could see all the skills I had worked hard to learn from my mentors, as well as the knowledge I had put much effort into mastering through coursework, now paying off.

Next, Michelle and I went ahead and organized our case studies. It took us approximately two months to conduct the data collection, complete the cross-case analysis, and write our preliminary findings. I did not realize how much work would be required to conduct original research. I discovered that I had taken on a highly labor-intensive project in the midst of finishing my coursework and preparing my dissertation proposal. Nevertheless, we managed to complete a draft of our paper just in time for the APPAM conference, which we both attended.

My colleague presented our paper. Fortunately, we were well prepared, and she gave a top-flight presentation. As for my part, I served dual roles as author and discussant for our panel. True to the standards of APPAM, we learned during the conference that our paper needed revising in two areas, the theory and findings. I listened attentively and appreciated this feedback. I could see where the insights of the other discussants, scholars in our field, were spot on. Despite these weak points, however, they assured us that if we followed their suggested recommendations, we would have a publishable paper and enough data to publish a few articles. Then, to our surprise, we were contacted by a professor who sat on the editorial board for a major public management journal in our field. He had read a copy of our paper that was posted on the conference website. He asked if we were interested in submitting our paper for a special edition of the journal that would be published about nonprofit organizations. Of course, we did not turn him down and we agreed to prepare the paper for this special issue. However, about a month later, we learned that the focus of the special edition had been changed, so our paper didn't fit the aim of the edition and we were not able to publish with that journal after all. Nevertheless, the fact that our research had sparked the interest of someone unrelated to our own program was a real eye-opener for us and, of course, very valuable to our academic self-esteem.

Later back on campus, my colleague and I discussed the comments from our session participants and the next steps for improving and revising our paper. We also decided we would conduct three additional case studies to strengthen our findings. Then an unfortunate twist in our collegial relationship occurred. My colleague and I could not come to an agreement about how best to revise our paper according to the comments from the APPAM. She did not agree with one of the changes we had been advised to make concerning the theoretical framework of the project. I believed that making this change was highly important, especially in light of the standing of the APPAM in our field. At this point, it probably would have been very helpful to have had a faculty advisor on hand to mediate the conflict between Michelle and me. Michelle might have been swayed by the opinion of a faculty member to adhere to the APPAM conference advice, and having made the necessary changes, I would have felt confident about pursuing the publication of our work.

Without such an advisor, however, and as the principal investigator and primary author, given my prior experience with publishing and my knowledge as a researcher, I could not allow our paper to be submitted for publication without these important revisions. I don't think Michelle fully realized that our names and reputations in our field were on the line. We had not yet completed our PhDs, and a negatively received publication at this juncture in our careers could very well have had negative consequences in our search for a tenure track position. Consequently, and unfortunately, we did not accomplish our second goal, that of publishing our conference paper.

The fact that we didn't publish our findings did not take away from the most important aspect of this experience, however. I had learned I was capable of managing a research project as a principal investigator while completing my PhD. The success of our research project had made two things very clear to me about my future: (1) I was very capable of completing my dissertation, and (2) I could successfully carry out research as a professor. Michelle and I learned that each of us was competent in conducting independent research, and with a little more insight into our situation, we could have published our APPAM project while completing our PhD programs. The opportunity remains to publish it, so in this regard, the opportunity to publish was not lost. In hindsight, the support of a faculty advisor probably would have been very helpful, but forging ahead without such support and being quite successful in this effort established my self-confidence as a researcher and scholar in my field at a level that nothing else could have achieved.

Looking back on my publication experiences while in graduate school, I see that it took time, focus, and effort, but the rewards that came at the cost of this additional stress were substantial. As a result, I feel like I transitioned from my identity as a dependent student to a mature researcher and career professional. I now look forward to going on the job market with two publications on my curriculum vitae, an achievement of which I am very proud.

CONCLUSION

The effort required to establish a publication record while in graduate school is significant, but doing so can be very rewarding professionally and also very valuable to your academic profile when you start your job search. The scenarios I have related here offer a small variety of the types of publishing that a graduate student can encounter while in school, as well as a sense of some of the difficulties and challenges that go along with the publishing territory. As I learned through my experiences, academic publishing standards are very high, and consequently, a great investment of time and interest is required in order to master the scholarly level of writing necessary for academic journal articles and conference presentations. Having a few publications in advance of starting the job search kept me from feeling overwhelmed, an experience that new PhDs often face when looking for that first faculty position with no publications on their curriculum vitae. In addition, the experts say that attempting to get published while navigating the job market, even for the most accomplished graduate students, is a challenge. Learning the ropes of article writing and publishing while also looking for a professorship can be extremely difficult to accomplish.

Based on my experience, I agree that the publishing process needs to begin earlier in the PhD student's tenure rather than later. Instead of waiting until your entrance into the job market is looming and you are under an acute time pressure to finish the dissertation, ensure that at least one article is published or under review before you start writing your thesis. Beginning the publication process early allows some time for a learning curve and for a more efficient graduation year. I can affirm that the experience of seeing one's name included on a list of career professionals published in a prestigious journal, while one is still in graduate school, is a worthy and rewarding accomplishment. Moreover, it can be attained in many different ways while completing a graduate program. I took the risk and stepped up to the plate and took advantage of the publication opportunities that presented themselves to me, and I also searched out places to submit articles or reports, efforts that can be part of every graduate student's program. Learning the art of publishing early in my PhD program helped me place a firm step on my road to obtaining a job in the professoriate and contributed to the groundwork of what I look forward to being my successful career in academia.

CHAPTER 9 GROUP DISCUSSION

Entering the job market with publications on your resume empowers you on a professional as well as a personal level. Therefore, as Leah makes clear, going the extra mile to get an article in print makes good sense. The writing process, especially for those not trained as writers, can be daunting. Many elements come into play when it comes to not sitting down to write. These can be a lack of writing skills, habits of procrastination, or simply low self-confidence.

Having a group discussion about the issues surrounding how to publish before graduation can be a good way to prepare for your first publication.

The video created for this chapter, titled *Make It Happen*, is about a student who needs motivation to write and publish. The video and accompanying materials for leading a group discussion on this chapter can be downloaded from the chapter 9 resource web page at http://dx.doi.org/10.5703/1288284315207.

CHAPTER AUTHOR PROFILE

G. Leah Davis, PhD

Dr. Davis was born in Los Angeles, California, and spent her formative years in Forsyth, Georgia. While in high school, she first set her sights on a career in health administration. After completing her BA in political science at the University of Georgia, she began a graduate program at Auburn University, pursuing a master of public administration (MPA) with a concentration in health administration. After graduating with her MPA, Dr. Davis worked for the Veterans Administration Medical Center in Tuskegee, Alabama. During this time she was awarded a prestigious National Association of Community Health Centers fellowship, where she worked as a healthcare administrator for Southern Illinois Healthcare Foundation in East St. Louis, Illinois. This work inspired her to pursue her PhD at Indiana University Bloomington in the School of Public and Environmental Affairs, where she was a double major in public management and policy analysis. She received a minor in information science from the School of Library and Information Science. Dr. Davis graduated with her PhD in public affairs and is currently pursuing her research interests in network management, social informatics, and policy in the public and nonprofit sectors.

Chapter 10

Life Beyond Graduate School

E. Shirl Donaldson, PhD

INTRODUCTION

What happens after graduate school? Most graduate students in a PhD program aim for tenure track teaching positions upon completing their degree, but not all. Knowing the range of career opportunities that exist for PhDs will give you other options if you are unable or do not desire to secure a teaching position. In learning about these other options, you may also find different and more appealing careers that you can then pursue. Putting your post-graduation plan together early in your PhD program will provide you with a goal that can keep you motivated when the going gets tough. Completing a doctoral degree takes time and effort and demands a skill set that includes planning, prioritizing, and performance. These skills and the PhD credential are valued and respected in many employment areas, so the career options are many, offering PhDs much freedom and choice. However, this wide spectrum of available opportunities can also make choosing a career difficult.

In this chapter, I will explore several career options available to PhD students, of which I became aware while putting together my own post-graduation plan. These options include academia, industry, and government. And I will also consider how these different careers affect lifestyle and finances as well as how they fit with personal preferences.

ACADEMIC OPTIONS AFTER GRADUATE SCHOOL

Before becoming a PhD student, I had a lengthy tenure working in manufacturing for a small company owned by my family that presented new challenges daily. After a while though, the pace and environment were no longer thrilling for me. On top of that, the customers for whom we developed our products had resorted to cost-cutting tactics to which they insisted we adapt our production methods. This made performing to our high standards quite stressful. As I was a new mom and didn't want to be totally stressed out with my baby boy, I began looking for new challenges in a different environment that was family friendly and more adaptable to motherhood.

Encouraged and persuaded by my coworkers, I started teaching business and technology courses as an adjunct professor at a local university that catered to nontraditional students. I mainly taught adults who worked all day and took classes in the evening, and I developed a great respect for these students' commitment to education and their willingness to work for a better life. Each class or cohort had various types of students. Some of these students were factory workers who aspired to progress to management. Others were already managers or lower level executives in insurance companies and credit unions who had maxed out their career potential without a bachelor's degree. Helping these people learn was fun and invigorating for me. There were a few instances in which some of the students actually knew more than I did about certain subjects because of their work experience. Teaching was helping me to grow as a professional and I enjoyed it immensely. Plus, the part-time evening educational structure allowed me to pursue my teaching career without completely abandoning my job with the family business.

The more I taught, the more I wanted to teach. This growing interest didn't seem like a problem, but on the occasions that I, out of curiosity, looked at the requirements for becoming a full-time professor, it became clear that I could progress only to a certain level in a limited number of institutions without a doctorate. I was already a wife, mother, part-time instructor, and business partner. I did not have time to pursue another degree. Then, my husband was inspired with a new idea for expanding our family business.

Like most entrepreneurs, my husband was always looking for his next opportunity. He found one, in another state, a thousand miles away. The oil and gas market along the Gulf Coast was booming. More machine shops were needed to make service and production components for the oil rigs and offshore derricks. Our previous business catered to the automotive market, which was slowing at this time and darker days were looming. This grim forecast gave us motivation to branch out, so we decided to open a second facility down in Louisiana. After much discussion, actually heated discussions including wailing and gnashing of teeth, my husband convinced me to help him set up the administrative and quality systems for the new location. It would be no sweat. I had created the systems for our current location, but I was trying to limit my direct involvement with our business so I could concentrate on my teaching. My husband and I made a deal. There would be a cost for my services: one year of my freedom.

We planned to relocate, and my husband and I agreed that after a year of further service to our company, I could have a full release from the family business to pursue doctoral studies. Louisiana State University, here I come! It sounded like a fair exchange at that point; but life rarely goes as planned. During this ramp-up and transition period, my husband traveled between the two locations every two weeks. He had other business partners and was grooming a staff at both locations. Then one day he went to a meeting with his partners in New Orleans. He always called me as he drove between locations and updated me on our "corporate progress." When he arrived at his meeting on that particular day, I could hear the other partners talking in the background and the exchange of greetings. He told me that he would call me back as soon as his meeting was over, which he normally did anyway to update me on any decisions that had been made. An hour later, I got a call but not from him. His partner was on the phone whispering to me. He wanted to know if my husband had been ill. I told him no and asked why. My husband's partner then informed me that my husband had collapsed in the meeting room, and that they could not revive him. My husband never regained consciousness, and I became a widow that day.

The traditional funeral arrangements were made over the next several days. Grieving and burial took place while I was still in shock. However, I was incredibly calm and able to make difficult decisions quickly. I later realized that the ability to function well during a traumatic event is a common symptom of denial. Eventually, reality would set in. Now what would I do with the businesses, the partners, the employees, the family, and the rest of my life? Would continuing at this pace garner the same results for me as it did for my husband? I did not want to drop dead at work one day in the prime of my life!

In the aftermath of my husband's death, I decided to continue with my plans to get a doctorate. I had to get on with my life for my son and myself, and this was the path that I chose. When I applied to the PhD program at Purdue University, I had been a widow for less than a year.

But I knew that my pursuit of more education would not only bring me closer to the goals I had before my husband died, but would also help me redefine myself as a single adult professional. I knew that a doctoral program would prepare me to become a full-time professor with potential job opportunities at a large variety of universities and would also open up several other professional options.

After successfully preparing for and taking the Graduate Record Examination (GRE), I applied to the PhD program at Purdue University. I had only been a widow for less than a year. Once I had completed the application for admission, and finally had been accepted into Purdue's College of Technology, I had officially become a PhD student. The application process was quite comprehensive, and that should have been a real warning about the program's intensity. Still, I dove in with all my energy and tackled the huge work agenda set before me. After completing three semesters of very demanding coursework and additionally challenging research during both summers, plus keeping up with my responsibilities as a parent, the thrill of the doctoral program was seriously waning. Fed up with graduate school, I wanted out!

One day when I was really tired of all the stress and overtime, I just decided that I had had enough. It had been a long day, long week, and long semester. I was exhausted. This was my second year, and I was reaching my saturation point with coursework, funding challenges, departmental politics, and teachers' pets of the highest level. I was in too deep to turn back yet still not close enough to the finish line. I did not want to read another article or write another analysis, critique, or resource justification. I did not want to draw another logic tree. I did not want to develop another concept map. I did not want do another "think, pair, share" active learning exercise. I did not want to participate in a group research project that required a final paper and a PowerPoint presentation for the third time that semester. The upcoming semester was bringing with it a whole new level of research obligations, not to mention the dissertation I would soon be starting, and now it was time to go pick up my son from school. On top of everything else, I had no idea what I was going to cook for dinner that night.

I went to see my advisor, explained to him my complaints, and informed the patient professor who was witnessing my meltdown that I was leaving graduate school.

"But where are you going? What will you do if you leave school now?" he asked in response.

"I don't know," I sharply quipped back. If I had known the answer to this question, I wouldn't have been in that meltdown state to begin with. The physical fatigue and the rigors of the doctoral program had severed my last nerve.

After a few days of walking around with my decision, eventually, I regained my composure and began to think logically, like a rational human being. Where was I going? Where *was* I going? My professor's question rang again and again in my head, forcing me to become more reflective and less reactionary. I had hit my PhD program midlife crisis. I didn't see it coming, but it made sense given that I hadn't entirely determined my career goals yet. I started to think about my original reasons for applying to graduate school and my long-term career goals. I knew I wanted to teach, but my program would give me a lot of other options as well, and I had never completely figured them all out. I needed a tangible goal within my reach to keep me motivated. I had to refocus and devise a strategy to lead me from the midlife crisis of my program to its completion.

The courses on my plan of study and my industry experience had prepared me to teach both business and technology curricula, but it was up to me to decide my teaching goals. As an adjunct professor, I had always been simply placed where I was needed. As a full-time professor, I could have more control over what I would teach, and now was the time to start focusing on my teaching goals. All I had to do was figure out what these goals were. Which courses did I want to teach? What type of institution would best suit my personality? Was I really going to be prepared to enter academia in a tenure track position? Whoa! Time to reassess!

I started looking at job postings on several of the education websites starting with HigherEd.com, the online newsletter. I learned which positions were available, the types of institutions that offered these positions, and how often they became available. Given that my work experience and education had equipped me to teach in both business and technical fields, I also had some other questions I needed answered. Would the pay be the same in both departments? Where would I be the happiest? Where would I flourish without getting bored after two years? After reading several postings for positions in which I would teach the conventional technology department or business department courses that didn't really excite me, I struck gold. I found a posting for a position in a department where business and technology were taught side by side.

I had found the perfect position for me, because it combined the curricula of both the technology and business fields and would allow me to leverage both of my areas of expertise for maximum benefit. This combination often occurs in the real world but not so much on college campuses. The job description was for a professor in a newly created entrepreneurial center in a large southern research university.

It was as if the job description had been written just for me. I could have been its poster child. I began to envision myself in a tenure track position in an entrepreneurial center. Many major universities already have one, and of those that don't, many are soon to get one. In addition to faculty positions, there are even postdoctoral positions becoming available in entrepreneurial centers across the country. Each of the positions I found in these centers seemed to be in alignment with my research interests, and the new pedagogies being investigated really excited me. I started to feel my old enthusiasm to teach replace my frustrations and anxieties with research and coursework. I remember thinking, "This is doable." I could make this happen and be in my element. In answering my professor's question, "But where are you going?" I had not only created a plan for my future, but given myself a reason to work through my struggles in the present. As a result of clarifying my career goals, I did not quit graduate school.

More likely than not, most graduate students will have more than one marketable skill, talent, or attribute. After I had found my dream job, I knew that I now had to build and manage my own brand as an individual and an expert in the entrepreneurial field. You can build yourself a brand as well. In doing this, your resume or curriculum vitae becomes crucial, both online and in print. It is a good idea to maintain various versions of your resume or curriculum vitae to better align with various job markets. These markets include academia, business, government, and social organizations.

ACADEMIC CAREER OPPORTUNITIES

Becoming a professor is the obvious first thought in terms of career paths for most of us pursuing a PhD. Fortunately there are various types of institutions, ranging from Research I institutions to teaching universities, community colleges, and junior colleges, in which we can match our personal interests and comfort level on the academic landscape. Some people will prefer smaller private colleges instead of larger universities. As an African American, I often consider teaching at a historically black institution. I feel a sense of obligation to connect and collaborate with these institutions, even if I am not directly employed by one. This would be one way I could give back to my community and share my knowledge.

Career areas can come out of the woodwork from places you don't expect them. For example, the first challenge I faced in my pursuit of a PhD was passing the GRE. I knew that a certain score was required to gain admission, which had me worried. My intelligence was not in question, but my ability to reflect this intelligence positively on a standardized exam was. The solution: I learned how to take the test. In teaching myself how to take the test with guidebooks and programs, I stumbled upon what was only the tip of a test-taking industry that serves the needs of test-taking students as well as sets up and evaluates the tests these students take. Teaching students logic and test-taking skills is only one sector of a huge assessment industry offering many positions to PhDs. The standardized testing companies employ thousands of experts in all academic subjects and skill areas to create standardized tests. Creating these tests is far more challenging than actually taking them. Writing test questions that adequately test the desired subject matter is a skill in and of itself. It requires a vast knowledge of the subject matter, along with psychology, statistics, and human performance. In concert, an entire sector within the assessment industry is based on scoring, analyzing, and validating examinations for students. Colleges and universities depend upon literally thousands of people to create highly specialized standardized systems to document student performance fairly and confidentially, as well as predict ability to succeed.

Organizations, such as the National Center for Fair & Open Testing (FairTest), are often cited by educators and those individuals affected by high stakes testing. FairTest, a nonprofit organization, seeks to increase the diversity of contributors and managers in organizations that produce, promote, and support the use of standardized tests. FairTest works to end the misuses of and flaws in standardized testing and to ensure that the evaluation of students, teachers, and schools is fair, open, valid, and educationally beneficial. This emphasis on diversity in test creation and implementation creates a demand for highly trained personnel who are members of underrepresented minority groups in research and assessment at companies such as Educational Testing Services and FairTest.

As mentioned earlier, the different academic job options available to PhDs offer a variety of career choices. Freedom of choice is very attractive to a recent graduate approaching the job market. As a solo parent, I have always thought that flexibility is important. After three years in a doctoral program, I have a new appreciation for freedom along with flexibility. Possessing a PhD gives a person that freedom. If you aspire to teach in higher education, every state in the nation is open to you. Unlike K-12 educators, a professor does not have to be licensed in each state. The PhD as a terminal degree speaks for itself. Your curriculum vitae becomes your calling card. Every state in the nation has at least two major Research I universities and several smaller colleges which focus more on the teaching of undergraduates. Depending on your field of expertise, the possible locations where you can work become almost limitless.

This freedom transcends geography, though. PhDs also have options in terms of the fields in which they want to work. Essentially, any field that relates to your expertise and draws on your skills in research, consulting, and writing is open to you. Generally speaking, PhDs tend to update their knowledge in their field and expand their knowledge into new areas of expertise concurrently, which continues to yield even greater opportunities as they advance in their career. Some of these opportunities are found outside the university. Most major universities maintain relationships with local businesses, industry, and government entities, so in many cases, these networks are already open for you whether you are a student looking for a future career or a current professor looking for extra income. For women, these opportunities can be especially attractive because they provide flexibility during pregnancies and the option to pursue part-time, adjunct, or non-tenure-track positions at certain junctures in life when family responsibilities or other obligations take priority.

NONACADEMIC CAREER OPPORTUNITIES

Once I had progressed further along as a PhD student, I became aware of several not-so-obvious career choices involving research, evaluation, and consulting. A research focused path obviously provides opportunity for the researcher, but research also creates positions for evaluators, assessors, project administrators, and program directors. There is a highly detailed and elaborate system in place to facilitate scholarly research and ensure credibility and quality.

Research can be sponsored by private or public entities. Many grants offered by these entities focus on pure research and development (R&D) in the traditional sciences. Research in engineering and technology tends to focus on problem solving and innovation. All of this research ultimately leads to an improved quality of life for society, so working in this industry can be very rewarding.

PhDs have the freedom to use their degree to obtain a career outside of academia or to enter into a variety of nonacademic industries to add an extra stream of income to their personal finances. The American dream is being redefined as the economy recovers and new industries emerge. Many professionals strive to enjoy multiple sources of personal income. Nonacademic opportunities, such as training, consulting, researching, and investing, bring a return on the time and energy invested to obtain an advanced degree and achieve greater financial security.

Corporate Training Positions — Training and Education

Corporate education and industrial training are critical for businesses in the private sector. Significant retraining programs are needed within industry for employees shifting into new jobs. Greater efficiency and competitiveness are demanded in emerging markets. Highly educated professionals with a broad spectrum of expertise are required to manage employee preparation, from needs assessment to program design and implementation.

My initial experience in teaching started in a corporate environment with employee training. I was responsible for training in quality systems and operations. Currently, my background in industry gives me a working knowledge of the ongoing training needs that challenge most growing corporations. Delving deeper into my program of study and exploring publications with advertisements for experts in my field, I am constantly learning of corporate and industry positions that require advanced degrees and product- or process-specific training.

Government Positions

Government positions available to PhDs are typically higher ranking administrative jobs or directorships in agencies such as the Departments of Homeland Security, Education, Energy, Labor, and Agriculture, as well as the Food and Drug Administration, Housing and Urban Development, the Centers for Disease Control, and the Small Business Administration.

The National Science Foundation (NSF) also offers several career opportunities for advanced degree holders. Many positions require a PhD or equivalent professional experience or a combination of education and equivalent experience in a field closely related to the areas managed by each NSF directorate. There are exciting opportunities for PhD holders to work as a program manager and opportunities for employment as a division director. A division director is responsible for overseeing and carrying out the day-to-day operations and management of the different NSF divisions. This includes working as part of the management team and advocating for program activities that promote the NSF's long-range goals and plans. Such positions offer individuals an opportunity to impact society directly, effecting change and assessing its results. These directors also manage resources to effectively nurture new and emerging science opportunities, as well as manage the support of existing projects.

Following 9/11, the term *national security* became a household word. People with expertise in identification, documentation, biometric data, and international standards are now in high demand. Not only is the technology of security new, but laws and practices to regulate the use of this technology are currently under construction. Experts struggle to define the line of demarcation where security is ensured, yet the rights and privacy of individuals are not eroded. Policymakers, strategists, and social architects working within governments and municipalities often look to PhDs working in think tanks to provide the expert information they need to craft policies for the new security technologies of our age.

Consultant Positions — Acting As a Free Agent

Consultants usually work on a contract basis rather than in a traditional salaried position. This means that as a consultant you determine your own schedule and can often fit consulting work in with a salaried job. Most universities often have language in their employment agreements allowing professors to work concurrently as consultants outside of the university while working as full-time salaried professors. Such agreements assume that the time constraints do not interfere with their commitment to the university and that no unmanageable conflicts of interest exist. Because academics can consult in addition to their traditional academic responsibilities, they have an excellent opportunity to earn extra income and stay technically current and relevant in their career-related field outside of academia.

HOW DO I LEVERAGE WHAT I HAVE LEARNED?

Having connections with a major research university makes it easier to stay abreast of newly developing trends in science, technology, business, and education. Many businesses and entrepreneurs need such expertise as they pursue innovation in areas such as green technologies and sustainability. When businesses and entrepreneurs pursue innovation, it presents PhDs with opportunities to teach, learn, and explore. Education and business collaboration stimulate and drive the economy, and such effort creates job opportunities that graduate students need to keep themselves informed of for the sake of optimal career planning.

Lifelong Learning

In considering what you will do once your education is complete, it is important to remember that learning is never really complete. It's a pretty safe assumption that most PhD students enjoy gaining new knowledge, and that is great. Though your goal as a student may be to complete your program and get a job, it is important to remember that once you have that job, whether in academia or not, maintaining your expert status will require you to keep gaining new knowledge. This is a lesson I have tried to keep in my heart and instill in my son.

I started my coursework in my doctoral program a few days before President Barack Obama took office. As my husband had recently passed away, I was now a solo parent creating a new life for my eight-year-old son and myself. Many of my friends were going to Washington, DC, to witness the first black president of the United States assume his responsibilities. I chose to watch the inauguration with my son at the Black Cultural Center on Purdue's campus.

My son had Monday off from school for the Dr. King holiday, and I had previously informed his teacher that he would be absent on Tuesday as well. We needed to be together. I took him to campus with me on that morning, and we spent most of the day watching commentary and the actual inauguration. This was a momentous occasion. America was starting a new chapter in its history, as was the Donaldson family. There are only a couple of people in our family with doctoral degrees. I was determined to become the next one. I wanted my son to look back on this day in later years and remember lessons of perseverance, faith, intelligence, and hard work. When he becomes an adult and people ask him, "Where were you during the inauguration?" I hope he proudly answers, "On campus with my mom, a new doctoral student in her forties."

I completed one degree each decade for two decades. I am now working on a third degree in yet a third decade. Life and personal situations motivated me to return to the classroom, and the more I learn, the more I realize the value and appeal of ever-increasing knowledge. The challenge to remain current is daunting but fun.

CONCLUSION

Students usually develop a true love of learning through the graduate school process. The quest for knowledge persists subconsciously even after formal education is complete. This unquenchable desire to continually learn is exhibited in avid reading, questioning of the status quo, and frequently asking, "What if?" PhD holders draw on this motivation to keep themselves curious about new developments in their field.

On a personal level, as I pursue my goals and passions, I've developed a different style of learning that has contributed to my growth as an adult. This new learning style has given me an opportunity to be a role model to the youth around me—not a model of perfection, but a model of continuous growth over decades. My example demonstrates that, rather than a chore, learning is a major component of a healthy lifestyle. As I gain experience as a faculty member, which will help me chart my course of success, I will be given the opportunity to assist students as they chart their courses of success. I have the chance to teach them the importance of lifelong learning to their careers and their lives.

CHAPTER 10 GROUP DISCUSSION

Once the PhD is in hand or in sight, the quest for the dream job begins. Shirl has described the landscape of opportunities available to PhDs, and the need to be careful about confining oneself to too narrow a perspective on career possibilities. Taking the wider view poses challenges, however, making it important to focus on the career you will find to be intellectually stimulating, enjoyable, and financially attractive. Greater appreciation and understanding of the major points in this chapter can be obtained through group discussion.

The video created for this chapter, titled *Options*, is about a new PhD graduate entering the job market. The video and accompanying materials for leading a group discussion on this chapter can be downloaded from the chapter 10 resource web page at http://dx.doi.org/10.5703/1288284315208.

CHAPTER AUTHOR PROFILE

E. Shirl Donaldson, PhD

Dr. Donaldson received her PhD in industrial technology from Purdue University in December 2012 and is currently a postdoctoral fellow researching entrepreneurship and diversity. A strong advocate of inclusionary practices in education and business, she encourages students to work to their strengths while constantly expanding their skill sets and perspective. She has mentored several graduate and undergraduate students in areas of progression and transition from undergraduate to graduate studies, research, and study abroad. Between her master's and doctoral studies, she served as an Industry Advisory Board member for two departments in the College of Technology. Her research agenda and commitment to intellectual growth is driven by her life experience. While completing her master's degree and for several years after, she worked in a family-owned manufacturing firm. She was married to an entrepreneur for sixteen years, and her family has owned other small companies as well. As a doctoral student, Dr. Donaldson served as a co-chair of the Technology Graduate Student Advisory Council (TGSAC) and was an active mentor of undergraduate students in the Louis Stokes Alliance for Minority Participation (LSAMP). She was recognized as an AGEP scholar and received a Purdue University Bilsland Strategic Initiatives Fellowship. She also collaborated in the creation of an innovation course and taught the initial offering. Today Dr. Donaldson's research interests include entrepreneurship, innovation, technology management, and diversity in STEM (science, technology, engineering, and mathematics) fields of study. She examines how academic and industrial environments enable effective learning, discovery, and realization of new and transferred knowledge.